About the Author

NOAH TALL is a longtime subscriber to *The New Yorker* and other magazines that people leave on their coffee tables when they want to look smart. He has also been a member of NAMES, the dyslexic branch of MENSA, since 1598. He is the author of the acclaimed national bestseller *The Tippling Point*, which has yet to be published.

BLANK

*The Power of Not Actually
Thinking at All*

Noah Tall

Harper

An Imprint of HarperCollinsPublishers

HarperCollins books may be purchased for educational, business, or sales promotional use. For information please write: Special Markets Department, HarperCollins Publishers, 10 East 53rd Street, New York, NY 10022.

FIRST EDITION

Designed by Nancy Singer Olaguera

Library of Congress Cataloging-in-Publication Data is available upon request.

ISBN-10: 0-06-087576-3
ISBN-13: 978-0-06-087576-3

06 07 08 09 10 ❖/RRD 10 9 8 7 6 5 4 3 2 1

To _____

Contents

THREE

General Custer's Little Big Plan:
Or, The Case for JSC (Just Say "Charge!")

FIVE

McKenna's Dilemma: How to Find Out What
People Are Thinking So You Can Take

SIX

Bang! Bang! You're Still Not Dead?:
The Delicate Art of Putting Holes in People

INCONCLUSION

Conduct That Funky Music,

BLANK

The Statue That Didn't Smell Right

In September 1983, or possibly July 1991, depending on whose version of the story you believe, a Syracuse art dealer by the name of Frank O. Gianfranco approached the prestigious Oprah Winfrey Museum of Fine Art in Cicero, Illinois. He had in the back of his SUV, he said, a marble statue dating from the second century B.C. It was what is known as a *kurio*—a life-sized Thracian figure of a nude goatherd standing with his left arm thrust out plaintively as though he is pleading with a tax agent or repo man not to take his beloved animals away. There are only about fourteen *kurios* left in the world today; there would be a lot more except no one can remember where Thrace was. Upon arriving at the museum, Gianfranco announced to its directors that he would part with the statue for either $10 million or a chance to meet Oprah.

Was this *kurio* authentic? they wondered. Or was it just a curio? Or even a mere curiosity? The museum's curator,

Garth Hebblegard, called in a team of top scientists from the University of Saskatchewan's Department of Very Very Old Statue Authentication. They spent three days examining the surface of the statue with high-resolution stereo-nuclearpolyencephalograms and really strong bifocals. They then drilled a six-inch hole in the statue and inserted a spectron colonoscopic microprobe, the most precise, as well as most painful, analytical tool known to science. The statue passed all these tests with flying colors, Hebblegard was informed. In other words, as the Saskatchewan team put it in their formal report, "The statue? It's *really* old."

Reassured, the museum bought the *kurio,* though not before Hebblegard shrewdly bargained the price down to $9.7 million. It went on display in the museum's Rigid-Antiquities-from-Improbable-Nations Wing and was a big hit with the public, setting a museum record of six visitors in one day. Reviewing the acquisition for *Cicero Today* magazine, the respected statuary critic, the statuesque Lynne Trogg, raved: "It's the thrill ride of the summer. If you see only one Thracian *kurio* this year, make it this Thracian *kurio.* Its raw, bruising sexual power will smash you into the back wall of the museum. Trust me, kids, this one's a keeper! Two big thumbs up and a falsetto whoop!"

The *kurio,* however, had a small problem. It just didn't smell right. The first to point this out was Delwood Snellbank, a postal worker whose job was delivering mail to the museum on weekdays. Snellbank usually arrived at lunchtime and ate a sandwich and apple while wandering around the exhibit rooms, observing the latest acquisitions. Even before entering the room in which the *kurio* stood, he gasped and exclaimed, "Ew, what's that awful stench?" A few steps closer, and he immediately declared the statue "repulsively odorous" and a fake. Authentic great art, he insisted, "don't stink."

Hebblegard tried to point out that Snellbank had taken a limburger sandwich out of his backpack just before entering the statue room and that might explain the unpleasant reek. Offended, the mail carrier stormed out, vowing never to return. Two days later, however, Madalyn Gargoon dropped in for a visit. She was one of the world's foremost experts on Thracian culture and in fact had just returned from a Carnival cruise to that ancient land, which she believes was located in what we now call Puerto Rico. "Hebblegard took me down to see it," Gargoon remembers. "He threw his arms out in a dramatic way and went, 'Ta-da!' And I said, 'What a piece of crap!' Well, the guy really got kind of nasty at that point." What did Gargoon see that made her instantly react in such a shockingly vulgar fashion? "I really don't know," she says now. "Maybe it was the New Balance sneakers. Most of your ancient Thracian goatherds couldn't afford that kind of high-end leisure footwear. But honestly, that didn't register on me until much later. Mainly, what I do when confronted by something complex like this is I close my eyes and take a wild guess."

Hebblegard was starting to get worried. A few months later, he took his friend, Peter Ficus, the former director of the New York Museum of Decaying Bric-a-Brac, to see the statue. Ficus is a noted expert on important stuff and a near celebrity as well, but he has always been plagued by acute ambivalence. So when he saw the statue, he had two opposing thoughts. One was: "Come on, he just doesn't *look*

Thracian. More like a Scythian around the eyes." The other was: "Wow! What a find! This was obviously sculpted by the young Botticelli in his college-prankster phase."

Now Hebblegard was getting more worried. He convened a special symposium on the *kurio,* composed of many of the world's leading experts on practically everything. They swarmed over the statue, peering closely at every inch of it, pinching its cheeks, tickling its armpits, chiseling off small chunks and tasting them, dripping strong chemicals on the surface and examining what reactions took place. After several hours, they all repaired to a nearby Mexican restaurant for dinner. There, a ferocious debate broke out. Half the experts pronounced the statue authentic and the other half denounced it as an egregious fake. A food fight ensued and after running out of appetizers and breadsticks to pelt one another with, the experts began hurling chairs and waitresses, some of them surprisingly hefty. More than a dozen people were hospitalized in the fracas, which cost the museum nearly $32,000 to defray medical expenses and replace damaged restaurant equipment.

Now Hebblegard was getting *really* worried. He realized that to safeguard the museum's reputation, he had no choice but to consult the ultimate authority. He wrapped up the statue and flew to Cleveland, where the *Antiques Roadshow* was appearing that week. After standing patiently in line, he was introduced to the show's on-air expert. Harry Monsoupolos of the respected Christeby's Auction House & Dealer in Fine Persian Rugs. As soon as he spotted the statue, Monsoupolos smiled broadly and his eyes lit up. "This is one of the finest examples of late-nineteenth-century Bavarian kitsch I have ever seen and worth as much as three thousand dollars," he told Hebblegard. "You are a lucky man to own such a treasure."

Defeated, Hebblegard returned to Cicero and auctioned off the *kurio* on eBay, receiving a $2,750 winning bid from Evelyn Farbisher, a retired schoolteacher in Michigan. In an interview with *Bidder's Digest,* Mrs. Farbisher later revealed that in making her decision to buy, she had taken exactly .003 of a nanosecond, an expenditure of brainpower roughly equivalent to that used by someone in a persistent vegetative state to twitch. Not only that, she had been distracted and annoyed during the critical decision period by the neurotic barking and nipping of her pet schnauzer, Edith. In contrast, when Dellwood Snellbank, Madalyn Gargoon, Peter Ficus, and the Mexican-restaurant combatants had appraised the statue, they all tried to use their eyes and look and then to use their minds and think, if even for a brief moment. But in .003 of a nanosecond—which for all practical purposes is exactly the same thing as not thinking at all—Evelyn Farbisher was able to outsmart the whole bunch.

Blank is about that .003 of a nanosecond.

1. The Evil Child

Imagine that I asked you to play a simple game. I place a three-year-old child before a board and instruct you to sit down and play checkers against him. Despite your advantage in years and weight, the child easily defeats you. I ask you to keep playing and the child wins again and again. He totally humiliates you, laughing derisively, pointing a finger and calling you a "doodoohead." What you don't know is that you are being subjected to a psychological test and the "child" is actually not a child at all but a brilliant midget. The real question is not which checker to move but how long it will take you to figure out that you're being gulled.

Dr. Felix Burnball did this experiment at Haverford College a few years ago and concluded that people who habitually think a lot tend to realize they're being conned only after losing for the thirtieth time, which is when the midget, bored, usually likes to light up a cigar. But Burnball found that those who never think and merely react to stimuli, much like an amoeba hit with a baseball bat, discover the ruse much faster. That is because these people take notice of their own unconscious physical reactions to the humiliation being dealt them, such as projectile vomiting or soiling their underwear. Before any mental activity took place, these nonthinkers *felt* something. They didn't have to bother taxing their brains. Just like Mrs. Farbisher who bought that sculpture on eBay mainly because her nose itched. And just like Harry Monsoupolos, the *Antiques Roadshow* expert, who later turned out to be an escaped lunatic from a mental institution and who eluded recapture only because he had to pee during the show and rushed to the bathroom just as the authorities arrived on the set to nab him, then managed to slip out a small window in the men's room. (By the way, it really *was* a Thracian *kurio*, it turns out. Hebblegard shot himself when he found out.) They *knew,* these people. Did they know they knew? No. But they knew something else, something nobody else knew. Which was that *nobody knows nothing*.

2. The Tiny Laptop in the Brain of Your Head

The part of our brain that leaps to conclusions that are reached without any thinking involved is called the *leapative concluder* or, in some circles, the concussive unconscious, because the unexpected hunches that suddenly slam into the brain of those who are receptive to unexpected hunches often feel exactly like being hit on the head by a heavy iron frying pan with a nonstick cooking surface. The study of this kind of decision making is the most important new field in psychology as well as the most lucrative for writers like me, who masterfully weave these concepts together into best-selling books with cute titles.

The concussive unconscious should not be confused with the now obsolete confusive unconscious made famous by celebrity psychiatrist and best-selling author Sigmund Freud. That was a dark, scary place filled with disturbing desires, fantasies, and memories such as having anal sex with your mother or roasting and eating your nutritionist and nobody wants to go down there anymore. No, the concussive unconscious is fun, like an expensive new laptop computer factory-loaded with great video games and PDFs of Angelina Jolie in the nude. It also processes data very quickly, the data we need to keep us alive. When you walk out into the street and suddenly realize that you've forgotten to put your clothes on, do you have time to think the situation over and consider your options? No, you instantly scream, "Oh my God! What the fuck have I done?" and you race back inside at top speed, hoping your neighbor the stalker didn't see you. Unfortunately, this is where my laptop metaphor falls apart because no computer will warn you when you're naked, but the principle remains valid anyway: the only reason humans have survived as long as we have despite our forgetfulness, laziness, and downright stupidity is because that tiny frying pan in our head hits us upside the unconscious when our conscious is goofing off. As the psychologist Richard T. Pilpel writes in his book *Don't Worry About It,* "The mind is asleep most of the time so you can't depend on it. But the concussive unconscious has insomnia, so it's up all night watching TV and will answer its e-mail if you send one. Or something like that. Don't bother me; today's my day off."

People are always warning us not to trust instantaneous reactions. They'll say things like, "Don't trust instantaneous reactions; they'll betray you and lead to a fiery, agonizing death. Instead, stop and *think*. Then think again. Then get a second opinion. Then rethink all that you have thought."

But what did you do when you bought this book? Did you do all that heavy thinking? Or did you just glance briefly at the author's name and say to yourself, "Hey, this guy's good! I'd buy anything he wrote"? Of course it was the latter. That was your concussive unconscious giving you sound advice. And aren't you glad you took it?

Of course you are. The first task of *Blank,* then, is to convince you not to think. Because thinking is wasteful, tiring, and unnecessary. But that is not *Blank*'s only purpose. I'm also interested in exactly *when* you should not think. Because there are times when you *should* think. Granted, these times are few and far between, but still they do exist. You will meet many colorful and interesting people in the chapters ahead—a champion golf coach, a great cavalry officer, a speed-dating champion, a man who eats nothing but linguine with clam sauce, and about twelve thousand more psychologists—and what all of them have in common is that they never, *ever* think. Except once in a while.

The third and most important task of this book is to convince you that the power of knowing without thinking is not some wild, untamable force of nature like the sex drive of Colin Farrell but a talent that can be nurtured, managed, and utilized in normal, everyday situations that will enable you to destroy your enemies, shove the slow and witless out of your way, and dominate your spouse. It is an ability that we all must cultivate if we are to achieve the important goal of making me America's all-time best-selling author.

3. A Better World in a Better Orbit

There are lots of books that tackle grand themes, that explain huge areas of science, history, the barbecuing of oxen, or some other immense endeavor. This is not one of them. *Blank* is concerned with the so-called little things, the "small" but truly important dimension of human behavior. Why can some people get away with double-parking while others are always ticketed? Why do we go to the bathroom so much? Why do we find people with bad haircuts so damned annoying? Why does going to the dentist have to hurt? Why do musicians always end up with the best-looking women? Is it possible to kill someone and not get caught? I believe that if we stopped thinking about such matters and just let ourselves go through the day in a completely thoughtless state, the world would be a better place. I believe—and I hope that by the end of this book, or certainly by the middle of my next one—you also will believe everything I believe and become more like me. Then we will have a better world. "I always used to think long and hard before making any decision, often calling in a professional philosopher to critique my logic before taking action," said Lynne Trogg, the woman who wrote that gushing review of the Thracian *kurio* earlier in this chapter. "Now I realize what a complete idiot I was. Not that that has anything to do with the statue thing. But it's all good. Whatever."

ONE

The Theory of Extra Lean Deli Slicing: How Knowledge Is Not Unlike a Fine Pastrami Sandwich

In 1997, Merv and Mona, a married couple from Fond du Lac, Wisconsin, arrived at an awfully clean laboratory at Vanderbilt University to visit a leading psychologist, Dr. John Godsense, the man who discovered that guinea pigs feel pain when you kick them. Merv and Mona were placed in a spare light celery–colored room (some thought it looked more like fennel) and were seated on two uncomfortable-looking plastic chairs. Electrodes were attached to the couple's ears, noses, toes, and genitalia. Eight video cameras were stationed around the room to record their conversation and actions.

Merv and Mona, who had been together since the second *Back to the Future* movie or possibly the third (they can't quite recall since those two films came out within months of each other), were instructed to talk about any topic that came to mind except the books of Ann Coulter.

They were then left alone with the videotape rolling. After a few minutes of conversation, they began to discuss what they were going to have for dinner later.

Merv: How about Chinese tonight?

Mona: *Ucch,* I'm so sick of Chinese, we eat it every Sunday.

Merv: I know, but I was really in the mood for some moo shu chicken.

Mona: I'm sorry, I just don't want spicy food tonight.

Merv: How about if you get some wonton soup?

Mona: How about I've been sleeping with Richard from your office since July?

Merv: Don't change the subject. Do you want the wonton soup or not?

This rancor continued to escalate for some time until they started calling each other terrible names and began strangling each other. Eventually, Mona hit Merv in the head with a fire extinguisher and four lab assistants immediately rushed in to separate them. Two assistants were injured in the fray. Moreover, one of the plastic chairs was upended, leaving the remaining assistants really annoyed because Dr. Godsense had always claimed it was an original Eames when in fact it was only from Ikea.

1. The Fat-Lip Lab

How much do you think one can learn about the state of Merv and Mona's marriage by watching the fifteen-minute videotape of their dispute? Can we tell if their relationship is healthy or unhealthy? I suspect that most of us would feel we need to know a lot more than just the fact that Mona kicked Merv in the groin or that Merv bit Mona's arm very hard at least six times. But, no, Dr. John Godsense has all he needs to know just by watching that little snippet of tape. He feels their marriage is in serious trouble and that one of them will soon be dead.

Dr. Godsense ought to know. Since 1978, more than three couples like Mona and Merv have passed through his clinic (which some have nicknamed the "Fat-Lip Lab" since they only accept people who have had too many collagen injections).

Based on his observations of these couples, Dr. Godsense has devised a sophisticated color-coding system (which he calls Irving, after his paternal grandfather) to define the range of twenty-eight emotions he has observed couples express. Rage, for instance, is puce, because nobody really knows what color puce is anyway and those who do, don't really like it. (Also, say it out loud; it just kind of *sounds* gross.) Anger is mauve, disappointment is chartreuse, crankiness is teal (because that's what Dr. Godsense's wife painted their guest bathroom three summers ago and he *really* didn't like it), mild irritability is safety orange, and feeling neutral is what is known in the home decorating field as *greige,* because, well, it's pretty neutral. Interestingly, no one has ever expressed a positive emotion in Dr. Godsense's office so he has not chosen colors for those emotions.

Over the years, Dr. Godsense has trained his assistants to detect these various emotions in his patients' eye movements, sweat volume, and, most important, hairstyles. As the videotaped version of the fifteen-minute conversation plays back, an assistant then writes down the various emotions observed every second until there are 513, because that sounds like a lot and any more would probably take a long time to analyze. So, for instance, the notation "puce, puce, mauve, teal, puce" would signify that in one five-second span, the couple was either having a very intense argument or that one of them was having a bad hair day due to awful humidity. Face it, humidity sucks.

The data is then ignored until the assistants stop laughing at the couple's misfortune and can compose themselves enough to act professionally. Eventually the results are given to Dr. Godsense, who is color-blind. Over the course of his experiments, a remarkable pattern has emerged: all of the couples who have been to the Fat-Lip Lab have either gotten divorced, filed restraining orders against each other, or sued Dr. Godsense for irreparably damaging their relationship. But not before Dr. Godsense has predicted, with a 58 percent accuracy, that each relationship would end.

How can he make such accurate predictions about a marriage after witnessing only fifteen minutes of interaction? Simple. He flips a coin and it usually comes up heads, which he says signifies, "Boy, are these two in trouble." The rest of the time he guesses. And that is where the most intriguing results lie. Despite the fact that Dr. Godsense and his team have a second-by-second analysis of a couple's marital DNA, he chooses to ignore the data and just wing it. This is what is known in advanced noncognitive study as "Extra Lean Deli Slicing." And as Dr. Godsense often tells his students, if you can't Deli Slice, you'll never cut the mustard in the psychology racket.

2. You've Got a Code in Your Nose

I watched the videotape of Merv and Mona with an annoyingly nerdy graduate student who pointed out that you could tell a lot right away by the fact that Merv was too defensive with Mona. Had he come out swinging right away, he explained, instead of just blocking her punches, Merv might have won on a TKO. Though neither Merv nor Mona showed any overt hostility during the session, other than extremely bellicose language and savage body blows, the grad student pointed out that Mona did roll her eyes several times (much as the grad student did during my visit), which he says indicated an underlying contempt, disgust, and hatred of her husband that she was incapable of expressing. Dr. Godsense's studies show that, surprisingly, these emotions are very bad in a relationship—unless both partners are Serbian, in which case it all works out beautifully.

"We had one couple come in here a few years ago," Dr. Godsense recounted to me as he fed sushi to his Japanese fighting fish. "They had been driving to Graceland and just wanted to use a bathroom. But we wouldn't give them the key until we had analyzed their marriage on videotape. Boy, were they pissed when they left."

One way to better understand how Dr. Godsense can predict marital discord is to use the analogy of what people in the world of Morse code call a "thumb." Why they call it that is unknown, but never mind. The story is told of how British military personnel in World War II were able to decipher the enemy's seemingly unbreakable code because Nazi telegraph operators persisted in sending their top-secret messages in a German accent. For instance, the Germans would habitually substitute the letter *V* for the letter *W*, transmitting communiqués such as "*Ve vill vin der var.*"

To the code-breaking experts in England's Bletchley Park, this was a dead giveaway that the message was being sent not by the French, the Poles, the Japanese, or the Italians but by the Germans! And once the British interceptors knew *who* was sending the message, determining which war the Germans planned to win and by what means took only a matter of years—mostly through trial and error, and by asking around a lot.

Thus, what Godsense is saying is that a personal relationship also has a thumb and when one partner places this thumb in the other partner's eye, a trained observer can easily read this signal and, through *isothumbic* pattern recognition, predict that a divorce will be forthcoming in weeks, if not days.

"In any healthy marriage the couple occupies at least two states," Dr. Godsense explained to me when I visited his lab with my then-wife. "For instance, I live here in Tennessee and my wife has a home in northern Florida. We see each other mostly on weekends and holidays. It works for us. Plus, did you see my assistant out there, the blond one with the space between her teeth?" I said that I had.

"Well, what Mrs. Godsense doesn't know won't hurt her. This won't be in the book, right?"

3. *It Was Open When I Got There*

Imagine that you are being considered for membership in my very exclusive country club. Ignore for a moment that the club has historically discriminated against people like you and that you don't have the $150,000 initiation fee we require. Are you the type of person we would want in our golf foursome? Would the guys in the steam room want to make mostly unfunny racist and homophobic jokes with you around? Would I want you talking to Mr. Tanenbaum's daughter at the pool? (You know, the one with the red bikini? The one who was smiling at me the other day? No, I wouldn't. So stay away from her.) In other words, are you the sort of person we would want to join our elitist organization so that you could then help us exclude others like you?

In order to determine whether you are worthy of joining our club, the admissions committee presents us with two options: First, we could spend months going over your financials, scouring your assets to see if you have enough money to pay our exorbitant greens fees, recarpet the men's locker room, and buy my golf buddies a round every Sunday. Then, after researching your net worth, we would interview your boss, longtime friends, and coworkers, as well as your pets. The second option is to spend thirty minutes in your bathroom to see what we can learn about you. Do you leave hair in the sink? Remember to put the seat down when you're done? (Little tip for you: if you're a man and you live alone, just leave the seat up.) Do you use what the guys on *Queer Eye* call "product"?

By now, I imagine that if you are not completely confused you have figured out that the first option would be a Thick Slice approach—somewhere between a slice of deep-dish Chicago pizza and a slice of New York Sicilian. The second option, of course, would be the so-called Thin Slice method. Almost like a chicken paillard that's been cooked in a little canola and salted to taste—and not nearly as bland as you'd think. But as we have already learned previously with Dr. Godsense, it is the Extra Lean Deli Slice that often yields the best results. Except when it doesn't. In other words, there is a third way to determine if we want you to join our club: we will send someone to break into your home, grab what we can in fifteen minutes, and then run like hell.

Somewhat amazingly, the once-eminent psychologist and now convicted burglary ring queenpin Dr. Chava Gander conducted such an experiment a year ago when she was a little short on cash. Dr. Gander, who is now serving four to six years at a minimum-security facility near Reading, Pennsylvania, asked her graduate students to interview twenty strangers using a personality test based on four criteria:

1. Desperateness. Do you have so few friends with obviously dubious credibility that you would actually listen to some graduate student explain an experiment?
2. Gullibility. Would you also be willing to give that graduate student your personal information? Say, your name, Social Security number, the code to your alarm system?
3. Optimism. Despite the fact that you are clearly a loser, are you a shut-in or do you still go out in the quixotic hope of making some friends? And if you do leave the house, around which hours will you be gone?
4. Taste. Do you spend your money on expensive kitchen equipment, art objets, and one of those flat-screen TVs? Oh, also, do you have an iPod—and not one of the minis, one of the big ones? Or are you the kind who just squanders your money on Internet porn and Cheetos?

Once Dr. Gander had compiled her data, she then had her graduate students interview her subjects' neighbors to get a more complete picture of their habits, their comings and goings, as well as whether they tended to leave windows open, had vicious pets, that sort of thing.

After roughly ten subjects had been successfully "profiled," Dr. Gander then sent her graduate students to these subjects' homes to ransack them for fifteen minutes—or until somebody called the cops. What her research uncovered was, as you might expect, not admissible in Dr. Gander's subsequent trial because the police had yet to recover most of it. But in the simplest terms Dr. Gander's experiment proved what John Godsense and his researchers have also known: the more we know about somebody, the more we can prey on their weaknesses. Also, some people who seem to have the worst taste in clothes, as well as the most appalling grooming habits, have the nicest things in their homes. Weird. And while you wouldn't actually want any of those people to join your chichi country club, you might want that fifty-two-inch plasma screen they own.

4. Listening to Doctors Listen to Impatient Patients

It's time we took the concept of Extra Lean Deli Slicing two steps to the right. Then two steps to the left, then once to the right, once to the left, then we're going to take one big jump backward, and finally two big jumps forward. There, you have just learned the bunny hop. But I digress. Research has discovered that patients only sue doctors they don't like, not doctors who are incompetent. (In fact, some patients sue doctors they've never gone to, just because they heard they were nasty and rich.) This carries some important lessons for the medical profession: First, patients are idiots and should be avoided. Second, if you must treat patients, don't spend so much of your crucial early training years memorizing names of bones, nerves, and organs. (And for God's sake, stop operating on cadavers—you can't save those people.) Instead, you should concentrate on improving your personality. Learn to smile a lot and pretend to listen to people complain about their "chronic back problems" and "Oh, I think I've been having lots of headaches. Do you think I have a brain tumor?" and "Can you give my husband something to make him less of an asshole?"

This more friendly approach all but guarantees that your patients will never sue you no matter how many forceps you leave in their abdominal cavities during major surgery. And even if you, say, Deli Slice the wrong kidney, you will receive a warm hug after the operation and Christmas cards every year.

Some years ago, for instance, my now ex-wife (who, by the way, I hear has been dating Dr. Godsense) went to an ear-nose-and-throat specialist. Never mind that she had broken her leg while skiing one weekend—I wanted to see how long the doctor would examine her before diagnosing the leg. After operating on her deviated septum—she snored a lot and always used to freak out that she was going to have a heart attack from sleep apnea—he sent her limping out of the office. But not before complimenting her on how her shoes matched her bag, and honestly, what woman doesn't want to hear that? But what was my point? Oh yes, the point was that appealing to someone's vanity can often make up for the fact that you have no idea what you're talking about. And may I say that you look very nice today?

Meanwhile, Dr. Ferenc Schmultzky, head of Atlanta's Schmultzky Center for the Advanced Study of Studying, has been tackling another aspect of the malpractice issue: the important question of why patients keep going to doctors they don't like in the first place. In 1992, Dr. Schmultzky conducted an elaborate experiment in which two hundred very sick people were sent to obnoxious, short-tempered imposters with no medical training whatsoever and two hundred completely healthy people were sent to real doctors who had been through twelve-step programs for improving the personality. These rehabilitated doctors now saw patients immediately and entertained them with jokes, songs, and magic tricks, sometimes even serving light hors d'oeuvres. Remarkably, Dr. Schmultzky found that none of the patients in the second group sued their doctors, while fourteen of those in the first group did. (The rest probably would have, but they died.) Obviously, Dr. Schmultzky decided, the reason people keep going to doctors they don't like is that they enjoy suing. It fulfills them, it completes them, it makes them whole. Dr. Schmultzky even devised a test by which doctors could identify these troublesome patients and give them certain injections that ended their miserable lives and made it look like a heart attack.

So the next time you're in a physician's office and he gives you a shot, and you feel your lips start to go numb, trust your instincts. And congratulations, you've just Extra Lean Deli Sliced that doctor. Unfortunately, you now have about twelve minutes to live.

5. Everybody's at the Deli

Just what is the secret behind Extra Lean Deli Slicing? And how old do you have to be to do it? Also, do you need a license? And what if you don't want to Extra Lean Deli Slice all the time because you want, say, some melted Swiss on your noncognitive thinking? Ah, but we are getting ahead of ourselves. The answer is that you couldn't escape Extra Lean Deli Slicing even if you wanted to. It's how we select one black sock and one blue sock in the morning. It's the reason why we channel surf late at night and settle on that *Who's the Boss* marathon. Extra Lean Deli Slicing is the impetus behind pressing the elevator button even though it's already lit. (Let it go already, the elevator's coming.) We all do it. Bird-watchers Deli Slice. Serial killers Deli Slice. Alien space invaders do it. Even birds and bees do it. Oddly enough, the only people who never do it are those slicing meats at the deli. It turns out that this requires years of study and practice. Oh well, there are exceptions to everything.

TWO

The Damp Basement:
Snap Goes the Judgment

Not long ago, one of the world's top golf coaches, a man named Brick Vaden, began to notice something strange whenever he watched a golf tournament. In golf, players are given a chance to hit the golf ball, a small white spheroid with hundreds of dimples, off a plastic device called a tee. The tee is ingeniously designed so that one end, which is pointed, may be embedded in the ground, while the other end, circular and slightly depressed, supports the ball, keeping it still and slightly above the earth's surface.

What Vaden realized was that he always knew when a player was about to miss or, in the colorful parlance of golfers, "fuck up." A player would draw back his club head for a drive, pause slightly at the peak of his backswing, and, just as he was about to make contact with the ball, Vaden would shout, "Oh, no! You're fucking up!" Sure enough, the player would invariably miss the ball completely, dribble it off a few inches to one side, or slam the club head into the turf, causing a piece of sod known as a divot to fly into the air instead of the ball. It didn't seem to matter if the golfer was a man, woman, or child, a pro or a novice, a Jew or a Gentile, though oddly, Vaden could perform his feat only when he was standing near the golfer, never while watching golf on TV. But annoyingly, Vaden didn't know *how* he knew.

Vaden is now in his early nineties and wears Depends. When he was young, he was a professional golfer, though not a very good one. But by using the name Arnold Palmer, whom he slightly resembled, he got many young women to sleep with him on the pro tour. Vaden is a short, angry man with the energy of someone in his late eighties, and if you were to talk to the neighbors in his Florida condo, they would tell you he used to know more about golf than anyone in West Palm Beach but now has forgotten nearly all of it. (They would also tell you not to play gin rummy for money with him because he cheats when keeping score.)

It is surprising, then, that Brick Vaden can call the outcome of a golf swing while not even paying particularly close attention to it—surprising, that is, to people who haven't read the earlier parts of this book and don't know anything about Extra Lean Deli Slicing or Thracian statue sniffing or the strange experiments of Dr. Chava Gander. You, on the other hand, have read that material and you're not a bit surprised, are you? To you it is so obvious how Brick Vaden accomplishes his golf-ball trick that I don't even have to bother explaining it. But the amusing thing is that *he* doesn't know. And it is driving him crazy.

"What do I see?" he says. "How do I do it? Every night, I'm lying in bed and I say to my wife, Ava, I say, 'Ava, it's torturing me, how I can do this thing nobody else can do. And what's torturing me even more is I got this great talent and I can't figure out how to make any money off it.' Of course, Ava never answers me. You know, she died twelve years ago, but I keep her ashes on the nightstand. Also I got a tootsie in 7B, Sheila Bobick—her late husband Bob was in wholesale jewelry—but she don't like to sleep with me no more because I snore so loud it keeps her up, plus she don't like to go too far from her oxygen equipment."

The stream-of-unconsciousness shouts that Brick Vaden erupts with on golf courses are what psychologists call moribund precognition. Such blank nonthoughts originate in a basement area of the brain where it is dark, scary, and damp, factors that can cause a stiff neck or aggravate a sinus condition. I think that is why we instinctively avoid going into that clammy basement. It's one thing to acknowledge the power of moribund precognition and Extra Lean Deli Slicing, but it's quite another to stumble around in a musty, evil-smelling underground space where your face might brush up against a nasty spiderweb or worse.

"My father will sit down and give you fancy theories to explain why he makes this or that decision," the illegitimate son of the billionaire Donald Trump has said. "But he's lying. And his books are all bullshit. I mean the reason he okays a deal is because it makes him erect. If it stays soft, he won't make the deal." That's moribund precognition at work.

It's hard for a lot of us to cope with the powerful truth that this is how most successful people operate. If a man goes to a doctor and asks whether the sixteen-pound tumor on his neck should be surgically removed and the doctor replies, "No, just give it a name and begin feeding it kibble," the man wants to hear sound medical reasoning that led to that advice. That man would feel nervous if, instead, the doctor just shrugged and said, "I got a vibe from the thing in the basement." I think that approach is wrong. Oops, sorry; let me rephrase that. I instinctively *know*—without thinking—that that approach is wrong. If we are to learn to improve the decisions we make, we need to stop trying to analyze everything and instead listen to that weird voice from the slimy, horrible creature in the dank basement. And then make sure we stay the hell out of its way.

1. Walking the Prank

Imagine that I'm a professor and you're a beautiful student who's afraid she's failing the course. I've asked you to come and see me in my office. You walk down a long corridor lined with photos of whales and giant squid mating in the ocean depths. You come through the doorway, take a seat, and adjust your posture in such a way that your short skirt hikes up and your long, shapely legs are shown off to good advantage. I rise, walk around, and sit on my desk so that I'm just inches away from you. I'm almost overpowered by the musky fragrance of your perfume. I can't help but notice the rise and fall of your ample breasts beneath your tight pink sweater as your breath starts to come faster and faster. My voice now husky and excited, I explain that I am going to give you a simple word test. In front of you is a piece of paper with a list of ten sentences. In each sentence, there is one word that doesn't belong. I ask you to remove those unnecessary words. Experts call this an unnecessary-word-removal test. Ready?

1. The wages of sin motorboat are death.
2. Have you been a naughty armadillo girl?

3. The man with the ax pizza looks very dangerous.
4. He says you violin once did him dirt.
5. He sidewalk likes to kill slowly and painfully.
6. He is wanted in six furry states.
7. He sentimentally seizes your throat.
8. You scream but no one can Popsicle hear you.
9. Blood is chinchilla oozing from many wounds.
10. The crime-scene investigator taco lifts a clean print off your purse.

When you first came into my office, you may have thought, or even hoped, that I was seducing you, but I really wasn't. What I did was play a little psychological trick on you. I've subtly altered your mental state so that you are now terrified that you're about to be murdered by a homicidal maniac. After you finished the test, you would have walked out of my office and back down the hall faster than you walked in. A lot faster. You may have even run, albeit unsteadily on your spike heels, because of the fear clutching at your wildly palpitating heart. Tonight, you'll probably have some awful nightmares—if you can even manage to get to sleep. With that silly little test, I actually altered your behavior. I made the laptop computer in the brain of your head—your concussive unconscious—worry about getting gruesomely killed. We best-selling authors can do that, you know. We are very powerful and we know a lot of neat tricks. I have taught you an important lesson here and in a subsequent chapter I may explain what that lesson is, unless I get a sudden impulse not to because I always go with my gut. Anyway, if you're bright, you'll intuit it on your own.

For now, let's just say this was an example of what

researchers call a *pranking* test. It was devised by a very clever and slightly sinister psychologist named Larry Goblet. He and others have done many fascinating variations of it, some of which led to lawsuits and investigations by university ethics panels. But Goblet remains unremorseful, even defiant. "Look," he told me recently in his office at UCLA overlooking the scenic San Andreas Fault. "First of all, I have the guts to peek down into that clammy basement you described so inadequately a few paragraphs back. It's more of a cave, actually. Secondly, it's boring being a researcher. You have to run the same test over and over and after a while you lose all your enthusiasm and you just start faking the results and going home early. Pranking lets us have some fun with the dorks who volunteer as guinea pigs and that keeps our morale high."

One of Goblet's associates, Libby Applefood, who is also his mistress, if the campus gossip has it right, staged an experiment in the unisex bathroom right down the hall from Goblet's office. After giving thirty student volunteers an unnecessary-word-removal test featuring a lot of water imagery, Applefood asked if they would like to excuse themselves and go to the bathroom. The effect of the test, coupled with the suggestion that they might need to relieve themselves, was enough to make the students feel a strong urge to urinate. But when they reached the bathroom, they found the door blocked by a prickly janitor who told them he had temporarily closed the facility to "remove a bad smell." (Actually, this was Goblet himself in a fake mustache and rented custodian costume.)

Soon dozens of students, many clutching their groins in real or imagined discomfort, crowded the hallway, mooing in distress. The idea of the experiment was to see how long it took before someone would step forward to organize his fellow sufferers into open rebellion and sweep the "janitor" aside. Amazingly, it never happened at all. After six hours, many of the students had simply urinated in their under-wear, while others had slipped into unoccupied offices on the floor and utilized wastebaskets or desk drawers. Only one student had managed to get inside the bathroom—by bribing Goblet with $40 and an heirloom Patek Philippe wristwatch that he still proudly wears.

Goblet gets annoyed when I mention it, but I find these pranking experiments disturbing. They make the prankees suspect that all of us, even I myself, are being constantly manipulated by psychologists, the government, the corpora-tions, the media, and various other powerful institutions of society.

In fact, we probably are. Free will is an illusion, I have discovered in my research, and most of us have become robotic zombies, kind of like the people in that movie, *The Matrix,* which really tells the truth but cleverly pretends it is fantasy entertainment. And like this book, which you are probably laughing at, thinking it's merely an entertaining diversion. In my next book, *Zombie Slave Nation,* I'll tell you how the system really works and who profits from it. If *they* don't kill me first.

2. The World's Fastest Date

At one time or another, all of us who are young, good-looking, and trendy have engaged in the peculiar modern ritual known as speed dating. I myself have done it hundreds of times, though, oddly enough, I've never emerged with a single phone number or even a smile, let alone an invitation to repair to the bathroom for hot, steamy sex. Oh well, just bad luck, I guess.

On a brisk winter morning not too long ago, two dozen men and women gathered in the back room of a Manhattan bar to engage in an even more peculiar ritual. It was called Really Speedy Speed Dating with a Touch of Extra Lean Deli Slicing, and was the invention of a leading psychologist, Dr. Alan Blakefarb. It was Dr. Blakefarb's belief that if prospective daters could make an intelligent decision about a member of the opposite sex in a six-minute speed-dating conversation, they could make an even more intelligent decision with no conversation at all, just by ten seconds of touching.

The participants were all young professionals in their twenties, a smattering of stockbrokers and lawyers and schoolteachers, as well as four tambourine-carrying Gypsies who came in a group from a caravan parked nearby. The beginning was awkward, with the men all standing on one side of the room, talking sports, and the women on the other side, dancing with one another and discussing which guys were the cutest while shooting shy glances at them. Finally, Dr. Blakefarb grew disgusted with the lack of progress and blew a whistle, ordering everyone to gather around him.

Each man would be blindfolded, he said, and get ten seconds with each woman. He would be allowed to touch her wherever he wished (although he could not remove her underwear) and to use only his hands and feet. After the ten seconds, a Chinese gong from the Han Dynasty would be sounded and the men would move on to the next women.

Dr. Blakefarb reports that the experiment seemed to be going spectacularly well until members of the NYPD's Felonious Sex Crimes Unit burst through the doors and arrested everyone in the room.

"If you enjoy fondling someone's erogenous zones, or having yours fondled, as the case may be," said Dr. Blakefarb, as he arranged bail at the precinct house, "the time goes quickly. If not, it's the longest ten seconds of your life. Sometimes, strange things happen at these events. Today, for instance, there was this Wall Street guy, an arbitrageur, who was attracted to one of those Gypsy girls. Well, as soon as he touched her, just a little pinch of her nose, she insisted that according to custom, he had to marry her, and her two brothers picked him up and carried him out the door with her running after. We all had a good laugh over that, I can tell you."

The popularity of Really Speedy Speed Dating with a Touch of Extra Lean Deli Slicing has been growing rapidly of late, despite the danger of police intervention. And it's not hard to see why. Everyone who dates is trying to answer one of two simple questions. For women, it's: Do I want to marry this bozo or can I land someone better? And for men, it's: How quickly can I get this babe to bed? Surprisingly, we need only ten seconds of touching to answer these questions.

Sharissa, for instance, a frequent Really Speedy Speed Dater, says she can tell a lot by the way a blindfolded man fondles her butt: "A lot of guys lose me right away by pinching hard or slapping. A guy who takes his time, who strokes my butt gently and lovingly while crooning 'Moon Over Miami,' that's a guy who's sensitive and kind and will make a good husband." On the other hand, Chaim, who claims to be a man, did not care for Sharissa, whom he had encountered at a recent Really Speedy Speed Dating event. "I'm a dentist," he said, "so I like to go right into the woman's mouth, because I can tell a lot by the quality of her dental work. I was checking out a filling in an upper front canine when this one woman bit me. She said she just got overexcited, but I think she did it on purpose."

So we can see that Really Speedy Speed Dating works. After all, Sharissa and Chaim weren't right for each other. But suppose I were to alter the rules just slightly. What if I made everyone try to look beyond their rather superficial explanations for choosing this or that hottie and try to figure out what's really going on deep in their complex, screwed-up psyches? Don't forget, the title of this chapter is "The Damp Basement: Snap Goes the Judgment," and I'm still kind of obsessed with that basement, even though the chapter is getting overly long. Is the damp basement just another of my show-offy, slick metaphors or is there literally a lethal, slimy ogre down there?

Two professors from Oral Roberts University, Myra Fensterwald and Luther Skittles, wondered the same thing and they have discovered that when you make people explain themselves, strange and troubling things happen, things that perhaps man was not meant to know. They're an oddly matched pair. One is a Mormon agronomist, the other an ambidextrous milquetoast. Myra is a man and Luther a woman. The only reason the two got into Really Speedy Speed Dating in the first place was to make a little extra money on the side because the pay at Oral Roberts is so low.

The two professors, as they are known on campus, run their speed-dating nights on the sly in the cellar of their home at 3:00 A.M. on Wednesdays because all dating, fast or slow, is strictly prohibited at Oral Roberts, except between married couples, and even then it must be chaperoned. Yes, you guessed it. *The event is actually held in a literal dark, damp, scary basement.*

At a recent session, Myra and Luther let me sit in and watch the fun, provided I promise not to put the moves on any of the female participants, which they claimed might skew the test results. Usually, in Really Speedy Speed Dating, the boys and girls simply pair off after the sanctioned touching is done and then go somewhere to have hot, steamy sex. But being professors, Myra and Luther insist that they fill out a short questionnaire afterward that takes about three hours, and also that they be hooked up by electrodes to a battery of sophisticated analytical equipment developed by the Department of Homeland Security to interrogate suspected terrorists. By the end of a session, then, Myra and Luther have reams of precise data on each participant's reactions to all that has taken place. When you examine that data, if you have any scientific background at all, the hairs on your neck begin to rise and the terror wells up deep in the pit of your stomach. But maybe that's just me.

At the session I attended, I paid particular attention to a young woman with pale skin, short, red, curly hair, and a really tight, low-cut top showing lots of cleavage. She looked very familiar. Finally, I realized it was Vera, my ex-wife, who had lost a lot of weight and dyed her formerly long, straight, blond hair. Of course, it was I who had tipped Vera off to the world of Really Speedy Speed Dating, knowing how desperate she was to snag a man, but I'd had no idea she would wander this far afield. I suggested to

Myra and Luther that they pair her with Utgar, an over-weight Mongolian hunchback with dirty fingernails, know-ing that she liked hairy men who grunt a great deal.

I thought they were perfect for each other, but when the Mongolian began to paw one of Vera's breasts with both of his enormous hands, she rolled her eyes in a way that I recognized, thanks to all the psychological research I'd been doing, as disgust, and tore herself from his clutches. Look-ing for a hiding place, she dashed behind the furnace, where a strange roar was heard, followed by a scream and what sounded like the crunching of bones. I thought I should mention this to the hosts, but when I tried to, Luther shushed me and pointed out the interesting interac-tion between another couple, Martha and George.

I watched them for the duration of their speedy speed date and it was clear Martha really liked George. She moaned shyly as George gently stroked her erogenous zones and several times said, "I really like you, George." It seemed like instant attraction. But let's dig below the surface and ask a question that may reveal the shocking truth that sometimes rests just out of sight where our eyeballs either fear to tread or simply cannot penetrate the sod. Namely, did George's personality match the type of man Martha had said she was looking for when she signed up for the session? Martha indicated at the start that she wanted someone handsome, sincere, intelligent, and funny. But George was an ugly, stupid, humorless wiseguy. Yet, she liked him! What's more, when asked the same question the week before, Martha had said she wanted a man who was effemi-nate, short, chatty, and superficial. "What does this mean?" I asked the two professors later in their kitchen. I had been unable to sleep and had wandered down there to pour myself a stiff glass of gin.

"It means," said Luther, fixing me with the saddest expression I had ever seen on any human being up until then, "that none of us can ever make up our minds about anything. It means we are a race of hopelessly confused idiots, ruled by chaotic, shifting emotions and neurotic impulses we don't understand."

"How do you spell 'chaotic'?" I replied, falling slightly behind in my notes. I was beginning to comprehend the nature of the knotty problem I was up against: how to organize the sprawling mess of diverse information I'd been gathering into a short, punchy book that could be described in one sentence to the buyer from Barnes & Noble. Also, I began to wonder why Garth Hebblegard, the man who bought the Thracian statue, and Lynne Trogg, the woman who wrote the gushing review of the statue, and Merv and Mona, the couple who fought in the laboratory, and the code breakers in England and the data-gathering Dr. Chava Gander and the screaming golf coach Brick Vaden and the pranking researcher Larry Goblet had stopped answering my e-mails and phone calls. On the other hand, I had gone into the dark, damp basement without thinking about it, followed my random impulses, and emerged unscathed, at least physically. I knew I must venture further. Perhaps I would even go beneath the basement.

FOUR

The Leonard Slye Blunder: Why We Fall for Squinty-Eyed, Singing Cowboys with Beautiful Palomino Stallions

Early one morning in 1931, at a Sunoco gas station in Duck Quack, Indiana, two men met when one cleaned the other's windshield with a soapy rag. The man with the windshield (at the time the windshield was the only part of the car he could afford) was a small-time grifter and cardboard-siding salesman named Earl Grobble. Passing through town on his way to nowhere, Grobble was a life-long failure (much like myself before I learned the secret mental powers I am revealing here in *Blank*), but he did not know it and thus was about to become a huge success. The other man, the one with the soapy rag, was an exhausted local who had been working three full-time jobs since he was a baby in a desperate attempt to escape Duck Quack, Indiana. His name was Leonard Franklin Slye.

Grobble glanced through the windshield at Slye and at that moment an idea came to him that would not only alter

American history but give me a chapter 4. "Milton William Slime," he said, slightly misreading the youth's name tag, "how'd you like to be king of the cowboys?"

Leonard Slye asked for a couple of years to think it over and then said, "Okay." A typical small-town fellow, he liked to spend his idle hours at the town cemetery, imagining what it might feel like to be dead. But the keen-eyed Grobble quickly sized him up as a gullible nonentity who was handsome enough—in a bland, nonthreatening sort of way—to be molded into a fabulous American success story. "Kid," he said, "hop in. We're heading for Hollywood, and I'm gonna make you the biggest singing-cowboy star in the world. From now on, your name's Roy Rogers. Think you can remember that?"

Slye did as he was told and Grobble was as good as his word. He taught the man now called Roy Rogers to sing and play guitar on horseback while shooting guns out of bad guys' hands. He acquired for Rogers a wardrobe of sequined cowboy outfits, a wife named Dale, a Jeep named Nelly Belle, and, best of all, a strikingly handsome palomino named Trigger. Sexually abused as a colt, Trigger had nonetheless emerged as an exceptional talent, charismatic, smart, priapic, and able to answer simple arithmetic questions by stamping a hoof on the ground, though fractions sometimes caused him problems.

Over the next fifteen years, Roy Rogers became the top singing cowboy in America. But Earl Grobble had even bigger things in mind and, in 1956, he arranged for Rogers to address the Republican National Convention in Philadelphia. "Roy," he said, "you're going to be president of the United States. I've fixed it with the boys in the smoke-filled room." Ever since the two had met, Grobble had believed that a man in a white

Stetson and riding a handsome palomino stallion could be president. "Most folks are not all that bright," he told Hedda Hopper, a leading journalist of the day. "They want a fellow who'll stand toe-to-toe with the top Commie, if it comes down to that, outdraw him, and shoot the gun out of his hand."

So Roy Rogers went from king of the cowboys to president of the country, because to Americans, he looked like the kind of two-fisted marshal who could impose frontier justice on a tough, unruly world. Though historians agree that he was one of the worst presidents in American history (he once ordered the army to attack the navy), they all give Trigger high marks for his foreign-policy initiatives.

1. When Deli Slicing Goes Awry, or, Watch Your Finger!

So far in *Blank,* I have talked about how powerful Extra Lean Deli Slicing can be, and how it gives us the ability to figure out what's going on before we've figured out what's going on. Dellwood Snellbank knew the Thracian statue smelled bad even before he saw it. Dr. Godsense knew the marriage of Merv and Mona was over before he even met them. Brick Vaden knew that his health care provider would refuse to pay for his Cialis prescription. Most of the voters who looked at Roy Rogers in the 1956 election saw only how handsome he was (in a bland, nonthreatening sort of way) and how he was able to shoot the gun out of the bad guy's hand and so they jumped to the conclusion that he would make a good president. They never stopped to listen to what he was *saying.* If they had, they might have noticed that he possessed a vocabulary of only twenty-six words, four of them obscene, which does not usually indicate an aptitude for complex presidential decision-making.

The Leonard Slye blunder is the dark side of moribund cognition. It's only due to my extraordinary integrity that I bring up this little problem because most authors wouldn't. They'd be scared it would undercut the whole thrust of their argument, confuse the reader, and mean lower sales. And yet here I am devoting an entire chapter to admitting that much of the time, the concept I champion doesn't work. Well, that kind of courage and confidence, right there that's the difference between a prizewinning, best-selling author and a mediocre hack.

What all of this means is that when I recommend that you give up thinking and just wing it, you'd better stop and think about it. I mean, I'm still for giving it up. I'm just saying it's your responsibility, not mine, so if you stop thinking and something awful happens, don't bother suing me.

2. Awkward Prejudices I Don't Really Like to Talk About

You've probably been wondering what the psychologists are up to, because I haven't mentioned them in a while. Don't worry, they're busy. A number of them have been looking closely at these unconscious, or implicit—also known as crazy—beliefs that help us take shortcuts to making up our minds when we don't feel like thinking. We all have built-in prejudices, even Nelson Mandela and Elie Wiesel. Maybe even Dr. Phil. Prejudice is the monster in the basement we met in chapter two that gave Vera such a hard time. (Turns out she survived, but minus a limb or two, and she had to spend six months in physical therapy to regain the use of her toes.) Much of the work in this area makes use of a fascinating tool called the FITB (Fill in the Blanks) test, devised by Sergei M. Luzhinski, Ngo Ming Li, and Mobutu Motutu of Rainbow University's Department of Diversity. The FITB test has swept through the academic world like a whirlwind to the point where, at many colleges, if you've never taken it, no one will speak to you and you can't get into a good fraternity or sorority.

Let me give you an example of one. The purpose of this test is to determine if you have any bad prejudices. This was the first FITB, so it is rather primitive and you should be able to finish it in less than two hours. You can use a pencil if you like, but frankly, I don't care for the idea of people dirtying up my book. So just take a finger and tap it in the appropriate column.

Lovely Person	No-Good Bastard

. . . . Jesus . . . .
. . . . That black guy with a knife . . . .
. . . . Tom Hanks . . . .
. . . . Greedy Jew with the big nose . . . . . .
. . . . George Washington . . . .
. . . . Mincing gay transvestite . . . .
. . . . Florence Nightingale . . . .
. . . . Michael Jackson . . . .

Oh, boy, are you a bigot! Okay, not really; I'm just teasing. I know you're really a good person, if a slightly neurotic one. But when you came to "That black guy with a knife," you really took a long time before answering, didn't you?

You knew it was wrong to assume that that black guy was a no-good bastard. After all, he might be a sous-chef or a Swiss-Army-knife designer or an Eagle Scout whittling a birdbath. But some long-buried impulse that you don't really understand stopped you from tapping "lovely person" right away. Even if you resisted the impulse, just from your long response time, the psychologists can tell you've got problems with stereotyped perceptions. Hey, it's nothing to be ashamed of. After all, we've been conditioned all our lives by ugly graffiti, Republican politicians, locker rooms at restricted country clubs, and the occasional Ku Klux Klan rally down at the shopping mall.

But that was just a warm-up. The next one's a lot harder. It uses pictures of randomly chosen faces to illustrate, once again, how we are often ruled by evil impulses we do not understand. For each photo, put a check mark next to one of the descriptions below. Answer really fast and don't try to cheat, because if you do, I won't respect you anymore.

Mild and trustworthy _____
Plays well with others _____
Honest and dependable _____
Kills when upset _____

Washed-up TV star _____
Short, older man _____
Angry black male _____
Needs plastic surgery _____

Looks familiar _____
Single parent _____
Angry black male _____
Starting to bore me _____

Busy homemaker _____
Angry black male _____
Needs to relax _____
Friend of Dick Cheney's _____

I told you it would be hard. I myself took this test three times and each time I became more confused and disturbed. I wondered, "Am I a racist because I identified every picture as an angry black male? Or am I just tired and in need of a good night's sleep? Or is this test rigged and the psychologists who devised it are really testing to see how quickly they can drive people crazy? Or am I an angry black male?"

3. The Tall Man in the Even Taller Hat

You put together the Leonard Slye blunder and the alarming results of the FITB test and what do you get? You get the TAVIACI syndrome, that's what. TAVIACI means the Average Voter Is a Complete Idiot. By a coincidence that can only be called extraordinary, it was discovered by Dr. Gaetano Taviaci of Vesuvio University & Pizzeria in Naples.

TAVIACI phenomenon was beginning to appear in American politics as early as the nineteenth century, although no one noticed at the time. Abraham Lincoln, then an ambitious young gay activist from Illinois, failed to impress voters until he started wearing a hat taller than anyone else's. Before that he was just another rail-splitter. No one trusted rail-splitters. You couldn't find an unsplit rail anywhere in Illinois and it drove people crazy. But when Lincoln bought a really tall hat, it brought out his height, which was truly impressive. The entire idiot vote went to him because idiots (as well as some morons and imbeciles and the occasional cretin) are impressed by tall men. Even then, the idiot vote was big enough to swing a close election. By the time Roy Rogers was elected president, TAVIACI was on a roll. Today, of course, TAVIACI is the dominant factor in American politics and both major parties base their nominations and campaign strategies on it and nothing else.

4. The Blind Leading the Blind

The sales director of Hummers of Ho-Ho-Kus, a Hummer dealership in the absurdly named town of Ho-Ho-Kus, New Jersey, is a man named Len Cephalopod. Cephalopod is in his fifties, with short, thinning pimples and wire-rimmed shoes. He bears no resemblance to Roy Rogers. He wears a bright red blazer and a straw boater so that he looks more like a bad actor playing a car salesman than a car salesman. But a car salesman is exactly what he is and he won't even try to deny it. On his desk, Cephalopod has a dozen Barnums, the award given every year by the World Car Salesmen's Association to the best car salesman in the world. In the world of car salesmen, Cephalopod is a car salesman's car salesman.

There are several reasons for Cephalopod's success, including the subtle but unmistakable hint of horrific violence implicit in his every gesture and expression. But more important than that is his refusal to prejudge a customer by appearance. "Most of the other car salesmen," he says, "they see some guy walk in here in stained overalls and a torn wife beater with blood and excrement smeared all over him and an ax in his hand and right away they assume he's a maniac. That's wrong. Today nobody looks like what they are. A six-hundred-pound brute in a dirndl with a swastika carved in his forehead could be a dot-com billionaire."

What Cephalopod is saying is that most salespeople are prone to making the Leonard Slye blunder. They allow their stupid, lying eyes to mislead them. They kick good customers right out the door with a string of curses and they suck up to penniless imposters wearing gold crowns and ermine robes. Cephalopod knew his eyes would steer him wrong. So he had them surgically removed. He decided to fight the Leonard Slye blunder even if it meant no more television for the rest of his life.

5. Think About Thinking About Thinking

How can we avoid making Leonard Slye blunders? We could choose the Cephalopod option, but that would ruin our basketball careers and, besides, we'd be bumping into one another all the time. The problem is that most of us don't know what we're doing when we're doing it. We learn about it only later when we read a book like *Blank*. And then it's too late. We've done it.

But we are not helpless before the onslaught of our bad

first impressions. There are ways to fight them off and kill them. "I had a student who used to hate Belgians," says Dr. Chava Gander-Guber, who has gotten married since we first met her in chapter one. "Every time he saw a Belgian, something in him curdled and he exclaimed, 'Yechhh!!' He knew he was a bigot and he didn't like it. So we devised a program to cure him of his prejudice. I went out and found a dozen drop-dead gorgeous Belgian girls and paid them to sleep with him. He found the experience so satisfying that subconsciously, 'great sex' became his primary impression of Belgians and loathing dropped down to number two. So now he still says, 'Yechhh!!' but first he says, 'Wowie!'"

In the next part of this book, I'm going to tell stories of four more people who successfully fought against the power of snap judgments. Or maybe three. We're running a little long. When you read them, you may think they were *unsuccessful*. But that's because you're making a snap judgment.

THREE

General Custer's Little Big Plan: Or, The Case for JSC (Just Say "Charge!") Decision Making

Oops, it doesn't always work.

Raise your hand if you noticed. Did you? Be honest. Yes, chapter four preceded chapter three. The reason for this phenomenon is grounded in actual science. Have you ever wondered, for instance, why the last four months in our twelve-month calendar have Latin roots that translate to seven (sept-), eight (oct-), nine (nov-), and ten (dec-), but are in fact used to name the ninth, tenth, eleventh, and twelfth months? Of course you haven't—because people haven't counted in Latin since MCMLXVI.

But here's an example I think we can all relate to. In 1987, Dr. Harry Harlem, a globe-trotting psychiatrist and the man who discovered agoraphilia, the intense love of shopping malls, gave fifty men and fifty women a simple test. He invited his hundred subjects to a two-day Sylvester Stallone film festival in which he showed more than a dozen movies, including the seriously underrated *Nighthawks*. Then Dr. Harlem also did something devious—following

afternoon screenings of *Rocky* and *Rocky II,* he had the pro-
jectionist run *Rocky IV,* and when it was over, not one person
in the theater noticed that the festival had skipped the vastly
superior *Rocky III,* which costarred Mr. T. in his prime and a
young Hulk Hogan as Thunderlips. In other words, Dr.
Harlem concluded, numerical order is meaningless.

Okay, I just made that last part up. The truth is I didn't
think about numbers enough. I was just concentrating on
the words. Which just goes to show you that you should've
followed your instinct to look at the concluding chapter to
get the gist of *Blank* and not bothered to read all the earlier
stuff. Better yet, wait until the book is reviewed and crib
your thoughts from that. Look, let's just move on.

1. Custer's Nightstand

George Armstrong Custer was a tall, lanky military man
with lustrous, fragrant blond locks that tumbled down to
his broad shoulders. Although he was a high-ranking officer
in the United States Army, he dressed in a fringed suede
jacket and a frilly, white-on-white dress shirt with a beautiful powder-blue silk bow tie ordered from the Sears catalog.
His friends called him "Custy" and "G. Diddy"—or would
have if he had any. Most who knew him assumed he was
gay, but he really just walked funny from riding horses a lot.

Once, when Custer was twelve, he was sitting in the
family outhouse in Ohio next to his father, who was reading
an old newspaper story about the Crimean War. "Well, son,"
the father said to young George A., as he made an entirely
different use of the article he had been reading, "that tussle's
about over. Says here the Brits is sendin' in the Light

Brigade." (The Light Brigade was the most glamorous military outfit in the world and had recently signed a contract with Matthew Brady for a book of exclusive photographs.) Right on the spot, George Custer decided that when he grew up, he would join the British cavalry and fight the Russians. Unfortunately, when he tried to enlist, he was rejected because his horse had flat feet. Also, he was a nitwit.

But Custer still longed to live in close quarters with other mustachioed men, to get all sweaty while training in tight-fitting brocade jackets and shiny black boots (or whatever was in fashion that season), and mostly to shower in groups. His dream was finally realized in 1857 when he was appointed to the United States Military Academy at West Point, where he distinguished himself further by finishing last in his class. Still, all who knew him back then agreed that no one threw better keggers or partied harder during spring break '58.

Upon graduation, Custer immediately joined the Union army in the Civil War, because he thought gray was a bad color for him. He rose quickly through the ranks, and in 1863 he became the army's youngest brevet major general, although he would have been less excited had he known that "brevet" was French for "probably be dead soon."

What distinguished Custer in those early years—besides being the only one in his regiment to own the chic Birkin saddlebag—was his remarkable decision-making ability. While other soldiers would carefully plot out their strategies, relying on the latest reconnaissance reports and those really big maps with lots of toy horses and tiny cannons, George Armstrong Custer had a different approach to war: he simply loved to yell, "Charge!"

It was a technique he had tested countless times in battle as well as in his dating experience. Once, during a pivotal moment in the Battle of Gettysburg, Custer gave a surprise order to attack shortly after "Taps" had been blown. That he had commanded his troops to burn down another Union regiment's tents was of some concern to his superiors, but Custer explained that they had been making too much noise at night and he wasn't getting his "eight hours."

The successful attack quickly established Custer as a courageous and decisive leader. "He may not always know who we're fighting against," Corporal Archibald Grant wrote to his brother, Ulysses S. Grant, in 1864, "but Custer always gallops, even when dismounted, and his looks are really smashing. Also, did you ever notice how you have the same name as the head of the Union army?"

Eventually, General Custer's men became so enamored of his fearless approach to battle that they often attacked without his order. On several occasions, they raced into battle, yelling "Charge!" because some wiseacre in another unit had sung out, "Da da da-da da daaaaa!"

2. One Morning Not Far from the Black Hills

In March 1867, a huge, elaborate war game was planned in North Dakota, because it looks a lot like South Dakota, where the Indians were making trouble. Here the army tested some of its most advanced technology, such as Gatling guns, bicycle regiments, and the new, experimental zipper fly. For the purposes of the exercise, the enemy was made up of U.S. soldiers pretending to be Indians. They were known, naturally, as the "Red Team" and were commanded by the army's strictest by-the-book officers. General Custer was put in command of the cavalry or the "Blue Team." Because the U.S. Cavalry was presumed superior to a bunch of fake Indians, the Red Team was made ten times larger and had access to all the latest intelligence reports, weather forecasts, and any bison sightings in the area, just to make the contest a little more fair.

But General Custer had something the Red Team hadn't been counting on: a really bad plan.

Nine years earlier, in the summer of 1859, George Custer witnessed a herd of berserk buffalo stampede a temperance meeting near a watering hole/spa in western Wyoming. When he finally stopped giggling, Custer realized that planning, thinking, and enjoying a hot bath before taking action were no match for pure, brutal instant aggression. (Additionally, he noted that red gingham doesn't really hide bloodstains or hoofprints nearly as well as he had thought.) It was then and there that Custer conceived his JSC (Just Say "Charge!") doctrine, vowing that the next time he was faced with a difficult military decision, he would simply go "all buffalo on their sorry asses."

So it was that on the opening morning of the war games, while the Red Team wasted time with such trite tactics as reconnaissance, cover, concealment, maneuver, and war dances, Custer, in a stroke of incomparable genius, simply attacked first. As soon as the war game started, his cavalry troop heroically charged the much larger Red Team, at the same time giving many rousing cheers, always the sign of a unit with superb morale. They were massacred. (While actual killing was not permitted, General Custer's men were given the war-game equivalent of death: the atomic wedgie.)

Bitterly protesting the referees' decision that his troops had been knocked out in fifteen minutes on a TKO, Custer blamed "hidebound conventional thinking that is resistant to fresh new ideas and is dumb, dumb, dumb." Unable to bear the shrill, high-pitched screaming any longer, the war-game judges awarded Custer a rematch.

At sunrise, Custer's Blue Team charged the Red Team— this time without weapons, so they could move faster—and once again they were swiftly "slaughtered." After the general had finished recombing his long, flowing hair, badly tousled by the wind, and touching up his makeup, he surveyed his weary troops. To a man, they had all been wedgied and, to add to the horror, not a few were pantsed. As their commander rode among their chafed and exposed bodies, they lifted their weary arms and gave him the middle-finger salute.

Two defeats in two days did not deter General Custer. Further demonstrating his penchant for bold ideas, he held the world's first press conference to tell his story to the public, convincing newspapers from coast to coast that he had in fact won the war game. As a result, Custer, now being mentioned as a presidential candidate, received the go-ahead from President Grant to head for South Dakota immediately and employ his new JSC strategy against real Indians.

3. Spontaneous Ejaculation

In a small basement in Upstate New York, eight amateur female comedians gathered for their weekly improvisation class. Known as the "Buffalo Jills" (I didn't think it was that clever, either, but I didn't have the heart to tell them), they practiced their craft for four hours each weekday evening in preparation for a show on Saturday night. As I sat watching them create mediocre, rambling skits without a script, it became clear that they were employing a fascinating comedic technique known as "Shouting Out the First Thing That Comes into Your Head."

I realized this when they asked me to suggest a title for their next skit, to be ad-libbed by shouting out the first thing that came into their heads. "Why don't you get real jobs!" I shouted back irritably, as I was concentrating on making new playlists for my iPod.

"Great," said Debbie, the leader of the Buffalo Jills and the one I was trying to sleep with to get over my bitter divorce. "So we have a scene called 'Why Don't We Get Real Jobs' and now we need a theater style."

Apparently Debbie and her group had not yet studied sarcasm.

"Kabuki," I said. The Buffalo Jills looked perplexed and started whispering nervously onstage.

"Um, none of us really know what that is," said Debbie. "Could you maybe suggest something else? We've only been doing this for six weeks."

"How about Pinter?" I offered. Blank stares. Crickets. "Forget it," I said. "How about—"

"We're really good at Shakespeare," one of the Jills offered up. "And the Farrelly Brothers."

"The Farrelly Brothers aren't thea— You know what, never mind. Just do Shakespeare."

"Okay, thanks!" said Debbie. "Wait, what was the name of the scene again?"

Now, had I been sitting in on a group of actual comedy professionals, I would have witnessed such classic improv techniques as "accept and build," wherein one member of the troupe must accept the other member's premise, no matter how bizarre or inane, and then build on it. For example, if you and I were in a scene in which you were playing a woman in a singles bar and I walked into the bar, you might look up at me and say, "Why, you must be Mr. Right." And then, accepting your premise and building on it, I might say to you, "Why, yes, I am. In fact, my brother Orville and I have just finished building the first airplane, and we'd like you to be the first stewardess."

Get it? The premise was that I was Mr. Right, but I just said the first thing that came to my mind and changed it to Mr. *Wright*. See, it's a pun. That's another comedic technique. Look, I'm not saying it's hilarious, but it's a hell of a lot funnier than those goddamn Buffalo Jills. And I never did get to sleep with Debbie, either, so give me a break.

4. But Back to Custer . . .

In the earlier section, I think I forgot to mention that while serving in the Civil War, General Custer had very significant and important experiences, often involving death, pain, suffering, and acid reflux. By not thinking much about them, by never asking piercing questions, and by looking really dashing in suede and other animal skins, Custer was consistently able to impress his superiors and climb the promotion ladder quickly. Or wait—maybe I did mention that. You see, I never look back as I write because that would slow down my intuition and leave me vulnerable to attacks of thinking. I'm sorry, I'm still kind of annoyed that I sat through three weeks of Buffalo Jill rehearsals and didn't hook up.

Where was I? Oh right, improvisational thinking. Custer. The point, as you have no doubt intuited by now, is that, like Extra Lean Deli Slicing, improvisational comedy is derived from the same noncognitive section of the brain as Custer's Just Say "Charge!" decision making. In 1992, Dr. Ian Plegg, the only person ever to receive a Ph.D. in Scientology, mapped out this elusive section of the brain: the infamous "third hemisphere."

While much is known about the left brain, where linear thought is processed, and the right brain, where creativity is derived, Dr. Plegg was the first researcher to discover this little-known lower subbasement hemisphere, or the LSBH. (Dr. Plegg would have won a Nobel Prize for his groundbreaking work, of course, but some of his more envious colleagues pointed out that "hemi" comes from the Greek meaning "half," and that technically you can't have a third half. But that's just the kind of left-brain thinking we're trying to avoid here.)

For decades, scientists dismissed the LSBH as an evolutionary fluke that had no function except controlling snoring during sleep. But thanks to Dr. Plegg's research, we now know that the LSBH will take control of the brain when the other hemispheres get overwhelmed with facts and shut down for a nap, because the LSBH is the only part of the brain that can run on AAA batteries. Whereas a person whose LSBH is in charge—a so-called LSBHian—may not necessarily function effectively, he will almost certainly be a lot less grumpy the next day and thus people will like him better.

5. Sick, Sick, Sick

On West Harrison Street in Chicago, two miles west of East Harrison Street, there is a huge hospital called the West Harrison Street Two Miles West of East Harrison Street Hospital. Built at the end of the early part of the middle of the next to last century, it is home to some of Chicago's sickest people. No one ever comes to Dirty Harry (as the hospital is called by its more sarcastic nurses) unless they are unconscious, because anyone with the power of speech invariably directs the ambulance driver elsewhere.

At least such was the case in 1996, when Dr. J. Newell Custer became chairman of the hospital's Department of Medical Intangibles. Dr. Custer, as you no doubt discerned with some Extra Lean Deli Slicing of your own, is in fact the great-great-grandson of General George Armstrong Custer, which means, according to some leading genetics experts, that he is a direct descendant of the famous general. This would explain the amazing talent for innovative procedures displayed by Dr. Custer.

On his first day at the hospital, Dr. Custer faced an enormous crisis. An outbreak of cerebral dermatitis had hit his small but insignificant Chicago neighborhood, and suddenly the hospital was overrun with patients. They were stacked atop one another in the halls and the basement. Some were even placed on gurneys outside the entrance, with the line stretching for miles. The delay was so long that one patient actually wrote a three-volume biography of Percy Bysshe Shelley while waiting for medical attention.

Springing into action, Dr. Custer (who tells women he chats with online that he looks like Noah Wyle from *ER*, but he really doesn't) diligently studied hospital procedures and discovered where the big bottleneck was: the doctors. It seemed they were wasting a great deal of time examining and treating patients. Fortunately, Dr. Custer had an extraordinary talent: he could determine a patient's condition simply by looking at him and saying five simple words: "So where does it hurt?" Stationing himself at the front door of the hospital, he processed each arrival in an astonishing twenty seconds, handing patients off to doctors with instructions such as: "Take out his kidney," or "Give him two aspirin and have him call you in the morning," or "Security, throw this bum out," or, simply, "Prozac." Though some critics groused about the hospital's sharply rising fatality curve, the Custer Algorithm, as it came to be called, turned the West Harrison Street Two Miles West of East Harrison Street Hospital into a model institution that today is often featured in the glossy pages of *HospitalStyle* magazine.

6. When Less Is Less

There are two very important lessons to be derived from the Dirty Harry experiment. First, the best decision making always comes about from Extra Lean Deli Slicing—except when it doesn't. Dr. Custer, unlike his famous forebear, did not rely on the Just Say "Charge!" approach to dealing with patients. (Although, if he had, he might have killed them off even faster.) Rather, he bravely ventured down to his LSBH, flicked on the light next to the extra refrigerator (the one that smells really bad because you forgot to take out those crawfish), and improvised. Put simply, spontaneity has a time and a place.

The second lesson, of course, is that Custers are morons. But you knew that already.

FIVE

McKenna's Dilemma: How to Find Out What People Are Thinking So You Can Take Advantage of Them Without Thinking

The young rock musician known as McKenna grew up in South Carolina, the son of immigrants from North Carolina. His father was a geologist who had hoped his son would also study rocks someday. McKenna missed that calling by only one letter.

When McKenna was a child, the family would gather around the stereo and listen to Madonna together. "My father loved her," McKenna explains, "because he had a huge underwear fetish. And when she was in her pointy bra phase, he was going through a similar thing. Actually, I'm not sure he'd want me to talk about that."

As a boy, McKenna had no real interest in music until a sophisticated uncle from the big city exposed him to an early album by the group Nine Inch Nails. "I knew immediately that I wanted to be nothing like that," McKenna recalls. His uncle Denny then exposed McKenna to an album by the Red Hot Chili Peppers, thinking he would enjoy the fact that one of the band's members was named Flea. When that failed to interest McKenna, his uncle simply exposed himself to the boy. The family doesn't like to talk about Uncle Denny much now.

Then one day, a neighbor took McKenna on a tour of his home and McKenna saw a poster of the Three Tenors. "Who's that?" the boy asked and was told, "I don't know. Some Italian guys. I just use that to cover a hole in the wall." It was this type of experience that eventually caused McKenna to learn to play the piano. That and the fact that his mother insisted he take piano lessons.

McKenna is short and wiry and has a head of hair that looks like a stalk of broccoli. People often tell McKenna that he looks like Justin Guarini, who was the runner-up on the first season of *American Idol*. McKenna is insulted by this comparison, however, because he says he voted for Kelly Clarkson that year.

After nearly a decade of piano lessons, numerous public performances, and a countless number of friends insisting he play a duet of "Heart and Soul" with them, McKenna entered a talent show. He placed nineteenth out of forty-eight contestants, which was fairly impressive because he later realized he had entered a dance competition.

At twenty-two, McKenna began writing his own music. His songs were difficult to classify at first—mainly because he was stealing other musicians' work and writing new lyrics. *"Who let the frogs out? Croak. Croak. Croak."* That's a McKenna song. Critics in the indie plagiarism scene couldn't decide: Was he actually a parodist, his generation's "Weird Al" Yankovic? Or was McKenna merely a *kleptoamnesiac*—the term copyright lawyers use to defend people who forget they have heard or read something before and inadvertently "borrow" another's work.

Within a few years, McKenna had abandoned writing songs with lyrics altogether and carved out a new niche for himself as an instrumentalist—a hard rock bagpiper. Using money from the civil suit settlement with his uncle Denny, McKenna cut a demo CD, *Let's Get Highland.* Unbeknown to McKenna, the demo was passed along to an A and R man at A & M Records in New York. It turned out the guy was actually a fraud, a total loser—in fact, he was just a cashier at the local A&P and had been claiming to be a music executive as his big pickup line. Still, it turned out that he really was the younger brother of the guy who was dating Elizabeth Ansell, a prominent executive at a small but successful independent record label in Manhattan. By her own estimates, Ansell receives forty or fifty demo CDs a month. "The majority of them," she explains, "come from my boyfriend's loser brother. He sends me about forty of the same CD thinking I won't notice. To tell you the truth, I put this one in by accident.

"The first time I heard McKenna play, though, it knocked me out," she admits. "It was like listening to early Günter Waldgrun, the hard rock glockenspielist. Just awesome." Then several weeks later, McKenna happened to be in an elevator with Michael Stipe, the lead singer from the very successful group R.E.M. "I really dig your music," McKenna said simply. "Especially 'Losin' My Religion.'"

"Thanks," replied the bald singer in the elevator, "but I'm not Michael Stipe. I'm Moby. Don't worry, though, I get that a lot."

The two men laughed off the misunderstanding and

then McKenna explained that he was also a musician and asked Moby if he could play a selection from his demo. Moby agreed, but only because he knew he was getting off at the next floor. McKenna was persistent and stepped off the elevator with Moby into, as it turned out, the reception area of his record label. After listening to "Kill or Be Kilt" Moby was so impressed with McKenna's music that he actually didn't call security. Instead, he telephoned his friend Elizabeth Ansell (whose boyfriend's brother is a loser) and convinced her to meet with McKenna.

A few weeks later, McKenna not only had a record deal with Ansell but had also cut a music video, which would have been a very effective marketing tool if MTV still played music videos. Ansell even got McKenna a gig at The Bottom Line, the legendary music club in New York's Greenwich Village. By 7:00 P.M. on the eve of McKenna's show, the line around the club was so long that the bouncers had to tell people to go home. It seems that people had camped out the night before just to hear McKenna play. In other words, people who know music—the kinds who produce records and the kinds who go to music clubs to discover new talent and hit on underage girls—were excited about McKenna's music. Also, they were promised free drinks.

"It really freaked me out," McKenna explains. "When I practice at home, most people tell me to 'keep it down' or 'shut the hell up or I'll call the cops!' or 'hey, asshole, take that cat out of the blender!' But now there were people lined up to hear me play. I mean, I thought I sucked."

It turns out McKenna was right. He did suck.

That night, Elizabeth Ansell hired Car Tunes, a research

company specializing in music people listen to while driving, to poll the audience at The Bottom Line. Car Tunes employees handed out response cards with a scale of 1 to 5, with 5 representing "I would definitely listen to this while driving" and 1 signifying, "I'd much rather listen to my eighty-year-old grandmother's books on tape." McKenna scored a -.820, which Car Tunes' statisticians determined meant, "I'd rather crash my car and die painfully in a fireball of twisted steel and glass than listen to this shit."

1. A First Look at Second Impressions

In her book *Why Are There Corners in the Oval Office?* political adviser Jennifer T. Hornberry writes about being on the campaign trail in the 1980s with then–Arkansas governor Bill Clinton:

> After one stop in Fayetteville, I was explaining to the governor that we have extensive polling for political issues such as the economy, education, reproductive rights, and other so-called "hot-button topics." The polling, I continued, formed the basis of his centrist doctrine when it turned out that his true beliefs were actually unpopular.
>
> "So what you're saying is," Mr. Clinton whispered to me in his raspy drawl, "that you'd like me to pole your hot button?" He cracked himself up with jokes like that.
>
> "No, sir," I said, rolling my eyes and removing his hand from my ass. "I'm saying perhaps we can use these techniques when you are flirting with women at fund-raisers."
>
> Now I had the governor's complete attention. "As I

see it, you always hit on women after giving one of your four-hour speeches. You're tired, irritable, not looking for hassles. And so you're willing to go back to your hotel room with the first woman who smiles at you."

"You know, *you* have a pretty smile . . ."

"Could you focus here, please?"

"Sorry. What are you saying?"

"I'm saying that instead of going with your base instinct, and bedding the easiest prey in the room, perhaps we could have a little poll." Mr. Clinton chuckled. "Don't even say it. I know, I know, *you don't have a little pole.*"

"Boy, you're good."

"I'm serious, here, Governor. I think we should narrow down your choices to three or four women and let the state troopers who guard you vet each one. This way, we may be able to weed out potential troublemakers should you ever decide to run for higher office."

Governor Clinton ignored Hornberry's advice, of course, but many people who worked with her in Arkansas (and later in the White House) said that she had much better taste in women than Governor Clinton did. Furthermore, Hornberry, whom many believed relied too heavily on polling, later went on to create the popular Web site amihotornot.com, which Bill Clinton visited frequently while president.

But what if these same polling techniques could be applied to music? What if gut feelings about McKenna's bagpipe album were wrong? What if Dr. John Godsense had reinterviewed those couples a month after their first visit? What if George Armstrong Custer had not yelled

"Charge!" on the Red Team until hearing back from his scouts? What if my ex-wife, Vera, had asked her friends what they really thought of me? That might have made a difference, right? (Okay, probably not.) What if you could get a second chance to make a first opinion?

The truth is, second opinions and polling can go only so far. And as we shall see, determining whether McKenna's music is any good may not require any Extra Lean Deli Slicing at all.

2. Sweet Smell of Failure

One morning a few months ago, I had brunch with two beautiful women in New York's Greenwich Village. Their names are Veronique Vache and Anna Fleming, and they are both dancers with the New York City Ballet. This has absolutely nothing to do with the book, of course. I just wanted to let you know that two attractive women wanted to go out with me. Nothing happened, but still.

A few weeks after that, I went to Armonk, New York, to meet Rupert Furrito, who owns The Ol' Factory, one of the premier perfume-testing companies in America. The thirty-eight-year-old Furrito is what is commonly known in the fragrance industry as a "nose." Based on his prodigious sense of smell and years of training—he has degrees in both B.O. chemistry and odor sciences—Furrito says his nose is so sensitive that he can identify more than 348 types of roses just by inhaling deeply. "I once detected the difference between a lima bean and a butter bean in some day-old chili in New Orleans," he boasts.

Each year, cosmetics companies pay millions of dollars

to companies like The Ol' Factory in order to create "the next big fragrance." Is there too much vanilla in Calvin Klein's Obsession? Too little lime in Bulgari's Green Tea? Furrito knows. Or more to the point, his nose knows.

Going to meet a man like Furrito is somewhat daunting. Although I don't wear cologne, would he be able to detect what kind of shampoo I use? Would he know what detergent I wash my clothes in? Could he tell what I ate for breakfast just by getting a whiff of my breath? "I have no interest in smelling you," Furrito said somewhat churlishly as I put my armpit up to his nose. "I don't really care what kind of deodorant you use, but I can tell you that it's not working."

Seven years ago, Furrito was hired by Chanel to reinvent its most successful perfume, Chanel No. 5. Since 1923, when the fragrance was first introduced by Coco Chanel, no perfume has been more successful, but in honor of the fragrance's seventy-fifth anniversary, Furrito was asked to "give it a certain *je ne sais pourquoi.*" After months of exhaustive testing (including one awful episode in which his nose could only breathe in and not out), Furrito arrived at the exact formula for his elusive new scent. The result was Chanel No. 6.

More testing was called for, and this time with people who were not experts. Some of them had allergies. Others hated "things that were French." One woman had even had a nose job, although she swore that it was just to repair her "deviated septum." Please.

Chanel hired focus groups to see how Furrito's new fragrance would be received by the public. The evaluators placed a scent strip with each perfume—Chanel No. 5 and

Chanel No. 6—in front of the focus groups. By now, I'm sure you don't care what the results are, but I will tell you anyway, because that's how I write these little parables. With more than 98 percent frequency, the groups chose Chanel No. 5, especially since Chanel No. 6 made most people throw up. Apparently, when creating the perfume, Furrito had accidentally written down "tuber" instead of "tuberose" and the whole thing smelled like bad potato salad.

Was this what happened with McKenna's music? Despite the experts' faith in his innovative sound, was it just like Chanel No. 6? Did it just stink?

3. "Hey, Bagpipe Boy, Your Music Blows!"

Elizabeth Ansell's company finally released McKenna's CD in 2003. At its peak, the album reached number 31 on *Billboard*'s Adult Contemporary Atonal chart. Or at least that's what everyone told McKenna.

So it turns out the experts were wrong. Elizabeth Ansell was blown away by McKenna's music, but she may have been whacked out on Quaaludes at the time. Michael Stipe was also impressed by McKenna's bagpiping, but it turned out he was really Moby. Even Rupert Furrito guessed wrong when it came to McKenna. While his focus groups were testing Chanel No. 6, Furrito played McKenna's CD on the stereo in the lab. He still thinks the CD is the real reason why the testers threw up. As he wrote to McKenna shortly after Chanel fired him: "Hey, Bagpipe Boy, your music blows! But please enjoy some Chanel No. 6 as a token of my appreciation."

SIX

Bang! Bang! You're Still Not Dead?: The Delicate Art of Putting Holes in People Without Their Minding

The 1100 block of Smoot Avenue in the Hawley neighborhood of Roosevelt Island is a narrow street of modest two-story garages and small, colonial-style factories. At one end is the bustle of Tariff Avenue, the neighborhood's noisy residential strip, and from there, things run downhill. Most of the homes on Tariff Avenue have an ornate facade of red brick. Unfortunately, there is nothing behind the facade because the owners haven't enough money to build anything more. They're proud but poor. In the late 1990s, the narcotics trade flourished in the area, but in the 2000s, the drug dealers found that managing hedge funds was an easier way to make money. In short, Hawley is just the kind of place where you would go if you were McKenna. And that is why McKenna made his way to Smoot Avenue.

I hope you haven't forgotten McKenna, the confused and somewhat pathetic musician from the previous chapter.

It was really an excellent chapter and I put a lot of effort into it . . . well, for me, anyway.

On the night of February 19, 1999, McKenna gave an impromptu street performance on Smoot Avenue, where it crosses Kellogg Street just below Briand Drive. It was his way of promoting his new CD, *Born to Be Tattooed*. He had fifty copies of the album in a shopping cart and hoped to sell them at $2 apiece.

But McKenna had made a tragic mistake. February, it turns out, is one of the coldest months of the year in New York—how could McKenna know that?—and Roosevelt Island residents are reluctant to attend outdoor concerts when the temperature is below 20 degrees Fahrenheit. Also, by the time McKenna had set up his sound system, it was 3:00 A.M., which in many working-class neighborhoods is considered a late start. It was for these reasons that the desk sergeant at the 347th precinct began receiving a flood of irate phone calls complaining that the eerie, haunting wail of an electric bagpipe was disrupting all attempts to sleep in the neighborhood.

A few minutes later, a blue-and-white, four-door 1998 Ford Crown Victoria sedan turned onto Smoot Avenue. It carried twelve large men armed with Glock automatic pistols, shotguns, Uzi submachine guns, concussion grenades, and a small mortar, but there was nothing to identify them as law officers except for their blue uniforms and badges, the word "POLICE" painted on the side of the car, and the flashing red lights on its roof.

Driving the Crown Vic, as such cars are known among men of low intelligence who watch *Cops* on the Fox Network, was Jimmy Taft. He was twenty-seven. Next to him was Bart Hartley, thirty-five. Seated on his lap was . . . oh, never mind. What's the point of naming all twelve?

It was Hartley who spotted McKenna first. "Oh, my God, I don't believe it," he said to the others in the car. "There really is a guy playing a bagpipe." Later, Hartley would claim that McKenna fit the description of a serial rapist who was active in the neighborhood. The rapist would stun his victims with bagpipe music and then, once they were vomiting, he would attack them.

Taft stopped the car, turned it around, and backed up until McKenna was underneath it. But McKenna kept playing, which Taft would later say "bothered" him. "I'm like, wow, something weird is going on here and I don't like it," he said. The twelve officers got out of the car, which took some time because their heavy bodies were wedged tightly inside. "Police," said Hartley, holding up his badge. "Please cease your unauthorized musical activity, sir, and come out from under the vehicle." At least that is what Hartley claims he said. An eyewitness later testified that what he heard Hartley say was, "Would you prefer to be shot in the pie hole or the asshole, motherfucker?"

McKenna had not noticed the police car until it ran over him and now found himself in a dark, confined space with the car's low underside making it difficult to keep his bagpipe fully inflated. What's more, his instrument's volume made it impossible to understand what the police were saying to him. "There was a lot of yelling going on," he would recall later, "and numerous obscene gestures, but I couldn't make any sense of it. Then I heard what sounded like 'Stop in the Name of Love' so I started playing that. I pride myself on honoring all requests. I have a huge repertoire, you know."

At that point, the police began firing. "We had no choice," Taft would later explain on *Charlie Rose.* "He was pointing those horns at us. In the dark, they looked just like muskets or blunderbusses and we felt fear, the kind of fear that starts in a man's belly and then seeps into every capillary, every lymph node, and finally into the very fiber of your being so that now you are no longer a man but a quaking, whimpering thing, a hollow shell drained of every quality that once made you human."

Ballistic tests showed that the officers fired 246 shots at McKenna, setting a new New York City single-victim nighttime record. Many of them missed him, ricocheting off the pavement to strike other officers or bystanders, but 193 bullets did hit home, opening gaping holes in McKenna's body, which let in painful quantities of cold, damp air. The bagpipe was punctured so many times that it began losing pressure and soon could no longer hold a tune. Fortunately, no one could tell the difference.

Miraculously, McKenna survived the encounter on Smoot Avenue, but he was never the same. Surgeons had to remove his torso and McKenna's HMO refused to cover the procedure, insisting that a simple appendectomy would have sufficed. His doctors informed the hapless musician that he would never play the bagpipe again, at least not the one he had been playing. He switched to the accordion and donated his old instrument to Bellevue Hospital for use as a colostomy bag.

It was soon clear to everyone in New York City that McKenna had been shot far too many times, and the police department was heavily criticized by community leaders and newspaper editorials for wasting expensive ammunition. "Sixty or seventy shots would have done the job perfectly well," wrote State Supreme Court Judge Plessy V. Ferguson in his decision in the case. "More than that is just showing off."

1. Stop the Music

Perhaps the most difficult judgment an ordinary person is called upon to make in the course of a lifetime is interpreting music in a tense situation. We hear music all the time. Music is an integral part of our everyday experience. It comes out of radios, iPods, people's mouths, and, if you define it broadly, the wings of insects rubbing against their legs. But what does the music mean? Why does one song make you hum along or tap your feet or even get up and do the polka while another makes you angry enough to shoot somebody, as in the case of McKenna?

Sometimes it is easy to parse a musical phrase. When General George Custer ordered his bugler to blow charge, the Native Americans arrayed opposite his cavalry troop quickly understood that Custer was in one of those dark moods of his and desired a good, cleansing spurt of violence. If I were to issue a shrill whistle while standing in midtown traffic, you would probably realize that I wanted a taxi and was not trying to serenade the passing cars and buses with "The Donkey Serenade" from Ferde Grofé's *Grand Canyon* Suite. Or say you run across Robert E. Lee and he is pursing his lips. You would be apt to guess, and correctly so, that he was about to whistle "Dixie." These are things that we just know. We don't have to think about them. They just come to us. We may not even want to know them, but there they are, anyway.

But other times, it is not so easy. Sometimes the cues are subtle. Say you are walking down the street and ahead of you stands a man playing a violin. The music has an ethereal, haunting beauty that easily transcends the most exquisite melodies you have ever heard. But the man is hideously ugly with a vicious sneer and piercing, enraged black eyes that carry a demonic threat. Can you afford to walk past this man without placing at least a quarter into the open violin case on the sidewalk before him? Or will he spring at you and smash his instrument over your head? It is exactly this type of situation in which your use of music interpretation is absolutely crucial to your continued survival. But some of us have no sense of pitch. The twelve cops in the Ford Crown Victoria on Smoot Avenue in the Roosevelt Island neighborhood of New York in the country of America had no sense of pitch. The judges on *American Idol* have no sense of pitch. Are such individuals doomed to tragedy and disaster? Must they always end up on *Charlie Rose*? Not if they master the new science of face speed-reading.

2. What the Hell Is Face Speed-reading?

I'm glad you asked because it just happens that I recently researched this fascinating phenomenon. The classic model for what it means to lose the ability to face speed-read is Krumholz's syndrome. People who suffer from Krumholz's syndrome have a perverse tendency to focus intensely upon the nose of anyone who is talking to them. They will slowly move their heads closer and closer to the nose until they are a half inch or so away and slightly below, so that they are peering up into the nostrils. As if this was not disconcerting enough, the Krumholz's syndrome victim will, if not deterred, comment loudly on whatever he sees going on *inside* the nostrils, often adding imaginary details. Besides creating embarrassing moments of the kind that cause most of us to cringe in shame, the nostril gazer also tends to lose the thread of the conversation, which can hamper him in the performance of his job or in his social life.

One of the country's leading experts on Krumholz's syndrome is a man named Lyman Lemon. Lemon does research at Betty Crocker University's Center for Krumholzian Phenomena, where he has devoted his career to studying one patient for the past forty-three years. The patient, whom I'll call Alvin even though it's his real name, is in his sixties. He is highly intelligent and can dress and feed himself, although he often needs help solving quadratic equations. The two talk every week. A typical session goes like this:

Lemon: Good morning, Alvin. How are you today?

Alvin: Great. Gosh, that's a big booger hanging out your left one.

Lemon: Last time, you mentioned you'd met a nice girl you seemed attracted to.

Alvin: It's kind of greenish.

Lemon: The girl, Alvin. Tell me about the girl.

Alvin: Her name's Marlily.

Lemon: Marlily. What an odd name. Very pretty, though.

Alvin: Not really. I'll bet it goes all the way back into your skull, that one. You really grow 'em long, Doc.

Lemon: Alvin, how did you meet Marlily?

Alvin: I'm amazed you can even breathe with that python jammed up your snoot. You better get that mother out of there before it suffocates you.

Lemon: Okay, try to focus on what I'm saying, Alvin. Tell me about how you met Marlily. And please back off a bit. You're making me uncomfortable.

Alvin: You know it actually quivers every time you speak? Sometimes it almost looks alive, like it wants to say something. Imagine the things it could tell us if we could understand booger language.

Lemon: Never mind the goddamn booger! Tell me about the girl with the stupid fucking name!

Alvin's nasal gazing is a perfect example of the havoc that can result when face reading fails. Alvin is a highly intelligent man with a graduate degree from a prestigious middle school. But because he lacks one tiny ability—the ability to stop staring up people's noses—he can throw even a mild-mannered professor like Dr. Lemon into a homicidal rage. Sometimes I think about Alvin's case and I wonder: What if I just left him out of the book? What if I delete this whole section? Would it really hurt the book? What is its point, really? I'll have to give this some more thought. Right now I just can't decide.

3. Timing Is Everything

In the movies and in cop shows on television, we rarely see the police running over bagpipers, stopping the car above them, and then opening fire. Instead they shoot at criminals played by thuggish-looking actors who are energetically shooting back. They kill the criminals. Then they stand around while crime-scene investigators with sophisticated instruments go over everything and find microscopic bits of hair and fiber that prove that the blown-away criminal raped and killed forty-six people in the last month. That is not the way it happens in real life. In real life, McKenna gets filled with bullets while playing "Stop in the Name of Love" under a police car.

The truth is that most police officers go through their entire careers without ever shooting a bagpiper or even seeing one, so that the few who do are completely unprepared for the experience. They are so confounded and mind-blankened that they might as well be Alvin peering up your nose.

For example, here is an excerpt from an interview with a traumatized police officer by Idaho State University criminologist Barbette DeBlaha in her fascinating book, *Peter Pepper Was a Piper*:

I saw the guy standing there and this monster had grabbed hold of him. My God, it was horrible, like something out of *Alien* or *Predator* or *Alien vs. Predator.* It had an ugly, misshapen sac-like body, sort of like a squid, only it was *plaid,* for Christ sake, and it had stuck its needle-like snout right in the poor guy's mouth and was sucking his brain matter out of his skull. And as I stood there, calling for it to stop sucking, it unleashed this terrifying screech that I think made my hackles stand up, though, to tell you the truth, I'm not really sure what a hackle is. I only had a second to react so I divided it up into two half-seconds, like we've been trained to do. In the first half-second, I thought, "Should I fire?" And in the second half-second, I thought, "Hell, yes," and I squeezed off twelve rounds. Well, I killed that nightmarish creature and saved the planet from being taken over by space parasites that would have turned us all into zombified slaves. I'm sorry I took out the vic, too, but I told his family they should be proud of the sacrifice he made for the rest of us.

As the number of serious bagpipe-related incidents rose in the mid-nineties, some of the more progressive police departments began instituting training programs to teach officers how to cope with such confrontations.

"What we learned," says Captain Brad Enwater of the Ramada Inn's Internal Security Division, "is that strange things happen when bagpipe music hits the human ear. First of all, time slows down, so that each excruciating note seems to last forever. Then, after about two seconds, the entire brain shuts down in self-defense and the thinking process then has to be handled by the kidneys, which are not really designed for that purpose. That is why people under stress so often void their bowels, because basically, that's all a kidney knows how to do."

Enwater devised an innovative training program he titled, "Stop and Think Before Killing the Bagpiper." It has now become the standard text for hundreds of police and security departments around the world and not a few music schools. "The crucial element in any police confrontation is time," Enwater told me by cell phone one day from the living room of his suburban home as I stood outside on the porch. "The longer the time you have to think about a given situation, the less likely you are to shoot somebody in the head. So we train our officers to leave the scene, have a few cups of coffee, read a good book or watch a ball game on TV, get themselves nice and calm and clearminded, and then—and only then—come back and shoot the bagpiper."

4. So There

So there they were on Smoot Avenue in the Hawley neighborhood of Roosevelt Island, near the bustle of Tariff Avenue: Taft, Hartley, the police car, and ten other cops. It was dark. It was late. They were scared. They saw a young bagpiper and he seemed to be menacing them. They couldn't hear his music well because they had a boom box and it was playing Kid Rock, but what they heard they didn't like. All twelve of their police minds started constructing scenarios to explain the unlikely scene before them. "He's an Islamic terrorist who's going to blow up the Fifty-ninth Street Bridge," thought one. "He's a cop killer who gets off on sneaking into the funeral parade of his deceased victim and posing as a member of a police fife-and-drum corps," theorized another. "I just fucking hate everybody," thought a third.

By the time all this scenario-constructing was done, the car had already run over McKenna, and the bump had disconcerted everyone inside. This was not the way confrontations played out at the police academy. The officers could no longer think clearly; their kidneys were in charge and the stage was set for tragedy as well as soiled underwear. This was the optimum time to adjourn to a diner for coffee and doughnuts and a long chat about whether the good-looking Latina babe in the precinct is doing it with the married lieutenant. But that never happened. It was too late. No face reading or music interpretation was possible. Instead, Hartley started shooting. And then Taft started shooting. And then policemen nos. 3, 4, 5, 6, 7, 8, 9, 10, 11, and 12 started shooting. And McKenna started bleeding. And finally, Hartley ran out of bullets. And so he did what any sensible person would have done in his place. He reloaded and started shooting again.

Conduct That Funky Music, White Boy

In 1982, the legendary conductor of the Düsseldorf Philharmonic Orchestra, Gustav von Schpritzenwasser, died in a hideous roller-skating accident. A young-looking eighty-seven, at least before his death, Von Schpritzenwasser was considered the greatest maestro in downtown Düsseldorf, but he was also a tyrant who often forced his musicians to play in the nude while he videotaped them.

Sensitive to accusations that Von Schpritzenwasser had hired only young, well-built male musicians and had favored the flute section, the philharmonic's board of directors decided to hold "blind" auditions for open orchestra positions to avoid any suspicion of prejudice relating to age, sex, race, religion, or breast size. They began with auditions for the conductor job itself. There were 1,379 applicants. A screen was set up around the podium so all could demonstrate their skills without being seen by the judges or the orchestra members.

Audition day dawned cool and dry with gusty woodwinds blowing from the northeast in the key of C-sharp. While the orchestra members waited, tuning their instruments (which I in no way intend as a euphemism for masturbation), the first candidate slowly made his way to the podium in near-total darkness, the lights having been turned out in the strikingly postmodern Düsseldorf Muzikanischer Konzertenhallmitgiftschoppen. This was Lionel Feppleganger, a seventeen-year-old prodigy from Frankfurt who was already being hailed by many critics as "the next Lawrence Welk."

Feppleganger began conducting, but the orchestra failed to respond to his musical cues. "There was something tentative about him," the orchestra's oboist recalled later. "Above all, a conductor must be able to clearly communicate his ideas to the musicians and he couldn't seem to do that."

Several hundred other applicants followed, and after four days without a rest, open rebellion was beginning to break out in the brass section. But then something strange happened. As soon as candidate no. 423 began conducting Bartok's little-known Gavotte for English Horn and Bathroom Plunger, a jolt of electricity ran through the room. The six judges, who had been slumping in despair, suddenly sat bolt upright and several clapped their foreheads and exclaimed, *"Holi Scheiss! Ist das nicht ein fabulozen Konductormann oder vot!"* One of them fainted.

Auditions are classic Extra Lean Deli Slicing moments. Trained musicians say they can tell whether a conductor is good or not just from his tie. And with no. 423 they knew from the first three notes. The orchestra members began chanting in unison, *"Vier, zwei, drei! Vier, zwei, drei!"* The judges rushed to the podium and tore down the screens, ready to proclaim no. 423 the winner, lift him to their shoulders, and parade through the streets while exultant citizens tossed *düssels* and *dorfs* in the air (an old Düsseldorf custom). But when the screens came down, there, standing on the podium, vigorously wielding a mop, was no one but Walter Schnerdlinger, chief janitor for the Konzertenhall-mitgiftschoppen.

Now cries of consternation filled the air. *"Ach du lieber, ich bin plotzing!"* said chief audition judge Werner Blutz. For he knew full well that being German, he and the other judges had no choice but to adhere strictly to the rules, which explicitly stated that whoever made the judges sit bolt upright and clap their foreheads must be hired to lead the Düsseldorf Philharmonic.

And so it was that Walter Schnerdlinger, janitor, began his extraordinary career as a conductor. What no one could have predicted was that this unlikely figure, standing on the podium in his green maintenance-staff uniform and waving a mop handle, would become a smash hit. Critics marveled that the orchestra was as good as ever and raised the old issue of whether musicians pay any attention to a conductor or whether he is simply a figurehead. But ordinary people did not care. Millions of Europeans flocked to Düsseldorf to cheer Schnerdlinger's every flourish and bought souvenir action figures of their hero. The man the German tabloids called *"Der Moppenmeister"* became a beloved figure who slept with all the most beautiful models of Europe, did a Diet Pepsi commercial, and ended up marrying Princess Caroline of Monaco.

I ask you as an objective observer: Does not this story beautifully sum up every point I have made in this book?

1. Ear We Go Again

Before the Schnerdlinger episode took place, orchestras had been notorious for treating janitors badly. They were underpaid, beaten viciously, and often kept locked in cages when they weren't sweeping floors or polishing banisters. But this was only one form of the rampant unfairness that plagued the world of classical music for many years. Because music is mainly ingested through the ear, hearing was glorified out of all proportion, often to the disadvantage of other senses. Many musicians regarded the ear as a sexual organ and treated it accordingly, while paying little attention to the genitals. Some even made a fetish of earwax, according it magical powers and wearing it in jeweled pendants hanging from golden chains looped around the throat. Walter Schnerdlinger, however, used his popularity to dispel some of these superstitions. He wrote and lectured all over the civilized world, and in Texas as well, and his ideas slowly took root. As a result, classical music is today a field in which boys and girls of any ethnicity can compete fairly and not be subjected to weird hazing rituals or nude water sports.

2. But Seriously, Folks

There is a powerful lesson in what some musicians and critics have called the Schnerdlinger Revolution. Why, for so many years, were symphonic conductors partial to Mozart and disdainful of Billy Joel? Why did they use skinny, effete little batons instead of the big, virile ones favored by drum majorettes? Why, for God's sake, why, did they stand with their backs to the audience, as though ashamed to show their faces?

Because they had not read this book.

And so they were doomed to misunderstand or fail to utilize the leapative concluder, the concussive unconscious, Extra Lean Deli Slicing, isothumbic pattern recognition, the bunny hop, moribund precognition, pranking tests, Really Speedy Speed Dating with a Touch of Extra Lean Deli Slicing, the Leonard Slye blunder, the FITB test, the TAVIACI syndrome, Just Say "Charge!" tactics, Shouting Out the First Thing That Comes into Your Head, the lower subbasement hemisphere, the Dirty Harry experiment, Krumholz's syndrome, and all the other concepts I have so patiently explained. They were unable to internalize the examples of Garth Hebblegard, Lynne Trogg, Delwood Snellbank, Madalyn Gargoon, Peter Ficus, Harry Monsoupolos, Evelyn Farbisher, the checkers-playing midget, Dr. Felix Burnball, Sigmund Freud, Dr. John Godsense, Merv and Mona, Bletchley Park, Mr. Tanenbaum's daughter (you know, the one with the red bikini), Dr. Chava Gander-Guber-Gerber (finally out of the slam and remarried), Dr. Ferenc Schmultzky, Brick Vaden, his late wife, Ada, the illegitimate son of Donald Trump, Larry Goblet, Libby Applefood, Dr. Alan Blakefarb, four tambourine-carrying Gypsies, Sharissa and Chaim, Myra Fensterwald and Luther Skittles, my ex-wife Vera, Utgar the Mongolian, Martha and George, Earl Grobble, Leonard Slye, Trigger, Sergei M. Luzhinski, Ngo Ming Li, Mobutu Motutu, Abraham Lincoln, Len Cephalopod, the student who used to hate Belgians, George Armstrong Custer, Dr. Harry Harlem, Ulysses S. Grant, the Buffalo Jills, Dr. Ian Plegg, Dr. J. Newell Custer, Noah Wyle, McKenna, Jimmy Taft, Rupert Furrito, Bart Hartley, Lyman Lemon, Alvin, Barbette DeBlaha, and Captain Brad Enwater.

You do remember who all those concepts and people are, don't you? Because if not, I've been wasting my time on you and I will become very cross.

Without a screen, Walter Schnerdlinger never would have gotten the chance to conduct. With a screen, his greatness was allowed to emerge. The first lesson of *Blank,* then, is: always use screens, especially in the hot summer months, when mosquitoes and other flying insects can make your life a living hell. The second lesson is when you have to make a really important decision, put it off as long as possible and then try to fob it off on someone else. If that doesn't work, just think about other things until your moribund unconscious makes the decision without telling you.

"When I have to audition a young actress," says famous horror-film director DuWayne Chevalier, "I don't put her on a soundstage in front of a camera, because that makes everything predictable. Instead, I have my assistant hide her somewhere in my home, office, or car and instruct her to leap at me when I least expect it and try to tear out my jugular vein with her teeth. That way, I instantly know if she is capable of conveying real horror."

When Walter Schnerdlinger went behind the screen on that podium in Düsseldorf, there were no janitors playing in any European orchestra, let alone conducting. Because everyone "knew" that a janitor could not conduct. But today there are hundreds and we are a better civilization for it. The screens had created a pure "Blank" moment, a moment when nobody knew what the hell was going on.

It is this type of moment, this concentrated burst of absolute confusion and mental panic, that we must learn to embrace and even cherish. We must trust ourselves to go blank at the critical junctures in our life and allow our better, unknown selves to leap into the void and act instinctively, even if it means risking a kick in the groin. I am told by a close friend who has studied with Indian holy men that one can achieve this same power through the mastery of Zen Buddhism, transcendental meditation, and bikram yoga. "But why bother," I asked him, "when you can do the same thing by spending fifteen minutes reading my book?" He burst into tears, realizing that he had wasted nine precious years of his life.

Now, having incorporated the lessons of *Blank,* you too can have the satisfaction of making your friends and relatives cry. And not only them, but often complete strangers. What's more, you'll never have a guilty conscience later because (1) you didn't think about what you did so how can you be held responsible? and (2) you were following the advice of a famous, best-selling author who has appeared on America's finest talk shows.

Together, we have journeyed through the mysterious terrain of the unconscious and learned the power of the snap judgment. Now it is time to snap the book shut and go forth to see if this stuff works in real life. Just remember that if it doesn't, you must be doing something wrong. You must be *thinking.*

Don't.